HOMEMADE ICE CREAM & GELATO

By Brian McQuade

Brian Eats New Hampshire: Homemade Ice Cream and Gelato
Copyright © 2019 by Brian McQuade

All rights reserved. No part of this book may be reproduced without the express permission of the author, except in the case of brief excerpts embodied in critical articles and reviews.

Published by Piscataqua Press
An imprint of RiverRun Bookstore, Inc.
32 Daniel Street
Portsmouth, NH 03801
www.riverrunbookstore.com
www.piscataquapress.com

ISBN: 978-1-950381-04-3

thank you!

Jessica for the idea to write the book. I'm not sure I'll ever write another, but I will continue the idea in video form with my YouTube channel.

My father Ralph for making me memorize and use words not in my normal vocabulary in my youth from the previous month's *Reader's Digest*. I'm not a wordsmith, but I do enjoy Grammarly telling me I'm in the 95th percentile or higher for vocabulary usage each week.

All of the amazing owners and staff who took time out from their busy schedules to speak about their most excellent ice cream with a guy who had never written a book before.

My friend Amber for giving the book a quick run through before printing and eagerly awaiting my reports on each trip for ice cream.

My great friend Ben for writing a foreword despite not knowing anything about ice cream and even less about New Hampshire.

All my friends and colleagues who supported me and looked forward to what I had to say about my latest adventure.

My awesome wife Tania for driving with me to different places, most of the time after we discovered her pregnancy and for giving every single one of my write-ups a once over before they went to editing.

My daughter Emmalina who I will have many new adventures with, some which will definitely include ice cream.

TABLE OF CONTENTS

PARLORS

KELLERHAUS / laconia	19
WALPOLE CREAMERY / walpole	25
18 DEGREES CELCIUS / north conway	29
MOO'S PLACE / derry	33
BEYOND VANILLA / hampstead	37
JORDAN'S HOMEMADE ICE CREAM / belmont	41
CREMELAND DRIVE IN / manchester	45
BISHOP'S HOMEMADE ICE CREAM / littleton	49
MEMORIES ICE CREAM / kingston	53
HAYWARD'S ICE CREAM / nashua	57
BRUSTER'S ICE CREAM / nashua	61
ILSLEY'S ICE CREAM / weare	65
LAGO'S ICE CREAM / rye	69
CONEHEADS / north woodstock	73
BOBBY SUE'S HOMEMADE ICE CREAM / freedom	77
THE MILL ICE CREAM CAFÉ AND FUDGE FACTORY / bristol	81
LONE OAK / rochester	85
GRANITE STATE CANDY SHOPPE / concord	89
DUDLEY'S ICE CREAM / loudon	93

FROM THE FARM

HATCHLAND FARM / haverhill	99
SANCTUARY DAIRY FARM / sunapee	103
RICHARDSON'S FARMS / boscawen	107
CONNOLLY BROTHERS DAIRY FARM / temple	111
SANDWICH CREAMERY / north sandwich	115

RESTAURANTS ("i'm hungrier than that...")

BLAKE'S RESTAURANT & ICE CREAM / manchester	121
ROSELYNN'S HOMEMADE ICE CREAM / epping	125
SMOKE AND CREAM / somersworth	129
THE COMMON MAN / multiple locations	133
SQUAM LAKESIDE ICE CREAM / holderness	137
SAWYER'S / gilford	141
ARNIE'S PLACE / concord	145
THE PURITAN BACKROOM / manchester	149
STRAFFORD FARM / dover	153

GELATO (...and, well, that's different...)

BUZA DAIRY BAR / concord	159
BLOOMIN' COW ICE CREAM AND GELATO / newmarket	163
SUB ZERO ICE CREAM / nashua	167
JAKE'S OLD FASHIONED ICE CREAM & BAKERY / nashua	171
MORANO GELATO / hanover	175
FRISKY COW GELATO / keene	179
CHRIS' WICKED ICE CREAM / milford	183

ALSO CHECK OUT THESE

THE ICE CREAM MACHINE / charlestown	189
SLICK'S / woodsville	191

Foreword

Ben C. Foster

I know nothing about ice cream. I know less about New Hampshire. So, when Brian McQuade asked me to write a foreword for his book on ice cream throughout New Hampshire, I completely understood why.

When I think about New Hampshire I have a flash, a television commercial plays in my head. Endless pine trees circle crystal bodies of water. A proud Moose appears from the deep wood, raising his mighty chest to gift an ageless song to the morning. His bold cry inspires the golden hawks to launch in flight upon a clear mountain filled sky.

The second flash I have is an inevitable anchor for my imagination. A vision of my every day. The New Hampshire that I work, live, and play in. My home. It's more than a holiday weekend destination. It's a place to live, but not always scented with pine or bathed in sunlight. One can experience a hard time living in New Hampshire, especially in February or March. The winters are cross. The sky can look and feel like a constant grey, with wind cold enough to cut. The highway snow has no Christmas magic left—just icy gravel with an occasional foam coffee cup, discarded by a morning commuter no doubt. The people are busy. No time for nonsense. If a stranger is among us, we stare. We study them. Make no mistake, New Hampshire residents have big hearts. So big in fact, their hearts need to be hidden at times. It's freezing outside. We keep them warm within, protected until needed. We are a proud working people who laugh, cry, and yell. We sing and we rally. We ignore and we fight. Like people in all places, we are a special breed, commonly unique. We are all just trying to get to Saturday.

New Hampshire is a beautiful place, though the winters seem to dominate our minds when organizing the current year's calendar. The weeks of blanket overcast can feel long and heavy, a burden that can seem unfair when anticipating spring and sun. The people bear it. We just want to get through the cold, through the Easter mud and onward to the earned promise of summer. We want summer, New Hampshire summer, the very dream outsiders envy. The television commercial that plays in my head. A place most green and beautiful. A place where the nights need to be spent outside. We, more than most, want to do summer things. With family. What are we doing tonight? Who's up for a drive?

I know nothing about ice cream. All families have stories that include it or surround it. My father's name is Randall, Randy for short. He often told us a particular story that happened in the middle of nowhere when he was young. This story was popular myth my father had ready if we ever asked what grandpa was like. My grandfather's name was Don. Don was the subject of many family tales such as this one. One hot summer afternoon, driving with all five kids in the wagon, Don uncharacteristically pulled off at a roadside ice cream stand. They sold five cent cones, and that was a deal too good to pass by. Pulling forward and stopping fifteen feet from the ice cream stand window, my grandfather remained in the driver's seat while the car remained running. Behind the ice cream window stood a teenager with a tall paper hat and a cream smeared apron, waiting patiently. He seemed happy for customers on that lonely highway. Five kids, five cones and one quarter given to Randy who was instructed to buy the ice cream and walk the cones back to the car. Randy proceeded. The request for the five cones was given to the teenager after the pleasantries were exchanged. He then proceeded to scoop, with purpose and professionalism. After two trips of ice cream delivery were made by my father from the ice cream window to the car window greeted by excited kids, Randy released the quarter to the teenager. A fast pause was shared, followed by the teenager in his paper hat and cream smeared apron, asking for two cents more. "Sales tax," he said.

With an understanding nod, Randy walked back to Don and asked him for the two cents. After an awkward stare and a raised eyebrow, a quiet low voice left my grandfather in reply, "Get in the car."

Confused, my father tried again to explain that he only needed two cents which was nothing. One of the other kids might have had two cents, being so little a tax. This time Don repeated himself in an even slower, lower voice, "Get...in...the car..."

While saying the words, Don glanced over at the teenager in his tall paper hat. Randy quietly said, "Ok...?" and got in the back seat with the rest of the happy kids, eating their five cent cones, all the while oblivious to the scene unfolding.

The teenager, only fifteen feet away and momentarily trapped behind the counter window and hearing all of this, started to yell. My grandfather revved his engine while gleaming coldly back at him, smiling the most devilish of devil grins. My father said he could faintly hear the teenager's diminishing roar, "You cheap son of a ...!" as their happy wagon peeled out and sped off from a cloud of dusty dirt and into the sunset. All to the happy music of ice cream and my grandfather's maniacal laughter.

I know nothing about ice cream, but I do know something about family—the company of players that surround your story. The gathering of this cast is something special. A family is something special. A line from an old Springsteen song comes to mind, "...nothing feels better than blood on blood."

Little reason is needed to gather. It doesn't have to be a World Series game or a birthday. The random nothing nights that will eventually get lost from memory are treasures. Sometimes gatherings can be as easy as an excuse to escape from the humidity. Escape from a normal Tuesday night. Escape from supper, homework, a bath and bed. Why not? No good news is on The News. The change jar in the kitchen needs emptying. Maybe a surprise is what we need to get through this week? Maybe a simple drive? Maybe we go for ice cream? Who's in? Some summer magic perhaps?

Maybe I do know something about ice cream.

What flavor of ice cream is Brian McQuade? He would tell you he's simply the most awesome flavor of chocolate ever tasted by man, but I'm not so sure. Brian can be quiet, easy to digest. A simple cone of strawberry or chocolate chip perhaps? Brian is a listener. His eyes read you as you speak. He studies people, ponders like an old man with a soft rum raisin, wondering how this rum raisin fairs with scoops from a fond memory. Brian has opinions. His choices are important to him and are not easily swayed. I have never met a more determined man. He might be a bold rocky road, or mud tracks with almonds. The missions he has chosen to pursue in his life may seem random to an outsider ranging from political aspirations for a better community to being a proud owner of a throwback vintage gaming center with a bright colorful sign that lights up the night sky, "McQuade's Arcade." A bubble gum sundae, maybe with rainbow sprinkles?

Brian believes in himself and in his dreams. After knowing him I can say...I believe as well. Brian has gumption, like cookie dough. Gumption. A word not heard much these days. He gets things done, keeps the plates spinning and the balls in the air. A drive in the car with Brian riding shotgun can be lonely when he is armed with a cellphone to call that guy or to check on that thing. Mocha Madness on a sugar cone could be him. Brian plays the piano, violin, ukulele, and has recently found his hand on the neck of a guitar learning its language. His love of Star Wars and the relatively new frontier that is podcasting has given him yet another wild west to navigate and contribute to. Brian is an explorer. He believes he can get there. Every day. No matter where it is. He believes he can. Brian just steps forward without fear. Brian will find Bigfoot. Maybe Brian is a thirty-three scoop party sundae, literally served in a portable kitchen sink with the whole gambit of toppings represented. Then again, that seems too easy. Maybe not.

Brian loves his wife, Tania. He met her on a double date with myself and my now wife of nine years, Acintya. Tania is cousin to Acintya and flew in to spend the week with us. One Saturday we went miniature golfing and needed a fourth. I called my roommate, Brian. He agreed and we all had a great time. That is where the boring part ends, now for the story.

After the miniature golf we went for ice cream. It was there, I witnessed Brian McQuade's almost disturbing obsession. Brian loves chocolate. I knew this already because the day I met him he told me, "Hi, I'm Brian. I love chocolate! "

Every day since, he has reminded me and anyone else within earshot, he loves chocolate. I didn't fully understand Brian's "problem" until this double date at an ice cream parlor with Tania, whom Brian had just met earlier that afternoon.

The four of us conversing pleasantly were finishing our desserts and I was looking to my left or my right for the waitress with our check. That's when I heard Brian ask Tania, "Are you gonna finish that?"

The question seemed out of place since at our table sat four empty dishes that were once filled with beautiful sundaes but were now consumed completely, or so we thought.

Tania, Acintya, and I looked down at Brian's index finger pointing to the bottom of her sundae where milky remains of ice cream had settled and pooled over a small, dark layer of chocolate syrup one inch over the dish's bottom. Tania let a chuckle escape in disbelief. Acintya and I silent, waited for the drop. Waited for the, "I'm just kidding!"

It never came. Brian just waited, pointing at the chocolate. Smiling, Tania slid the dish over as Brian eagerly accepted it, sharing her smile. The milky remains of a once proud dessert from a total stranger were now being eaten among shocked friends. Brian LOVES chocolate! For the first time, I truly believed him.

Among all of Brian's hobbies, pursuits and interests I feel the one collection he has nurtured that I envy the most is his proud gallery of friends. He wants to know people. It is a talent. Remembering not only their names but always something unique about them. Always addressing people with familiarity, even if he has only met them once or twice. Brian wants to know you. He likes people. Dismisses no one. Maybe Brian is a

Lemon Cream or a Vanilla Bean. Could he be vanilla, a flavor that waits ready, for a variety of toppings or crumbles completing different and exciting relationships? Brian may be the scoop that accessorizes or improves a warm brownie or fresh peach pie. Maybe?

I do know that if people were flavors listed at a roadside ice cream stand, Brian would have the hardest time making a decision. He loves all flavors of people.

When I heard from Brian about his ice cream book showcasing the flavors, places, and people within this wonderful state of New Hampshire I wasn't surprised. It sounded like an adventure. It sounded fun. Sweet, familiar, and soothing. Which is why we come back to things we love. A summer sunset behind a gravel walk up. A chalk sign with tonight's special assortments. Would you like a sample? Hot fudge? Don't forget the tip jar. Not too buggy tonight. These cones are big! Don't drop it now.

Music plays from a car. Nick Drake's "Pink Moon" escapes from a window half down. First dates are happening. New families. Shy elders watch and remember. Puppies on leashes. People we love. Things we need. Things like chocolate. For me, people like Brian. I know nothing about ice cream or New Hampshire, but I do know something about Brian McQuade.

So when he asked me to write a foreword for his book on ice cream throughout New Hampshire, I completely understood why. The world needs to know that he is simply the most awesome flavor of chocolate ever tasted by man.

definitions

BASE – Ok, so this is weird. Generally speaking, the ice cream base is considered the ingredients used to create your ice cream pre-flavoring. This almost always includes sugar, cream, and eggs but can vary depending on recipe. On my adventure throughout the state though, it was clear to me that more than a few people thought I was asking about their flavors made from scratch when I mentioned the word "base." It happened often enough to make me question the very meaning of the word. I believe I avoided using the word when talking about flavors made from scratch. If I missed a spot or two, sorry, it's been four months, I wouldn't be surprised if I missed something. Flavorings can be from a distributor such as Oringer or I. Rice or made from scratch, which I will indicate throughout the book.

OVERRUN – This is a term used to describe how much air is pushed into the ice cream as it's being made. It's important for numerous reasons including the taste and texture of the product as well as profit margin. I try to avoid using the word in the book, but just so you know, it's a thing.

HOMEMADE – This is a term that has a wide range of definitions. For the purposes of this book, it will be used in the broadest sense. Any ice cream parlor that mixes a base with flavors can and does consider themselves homemade. All places in this book are considered homemade.

BATCH FREEZER – A batch freezer is a machine that produces large amounts of ice cream by mixing and freezing the base mix and flavoring at the same time.

introduction

I prefer hard serve to soft serve ice cream, but there is something to be said about the stage where ice cream isn't hard, but isn't a milkshake either. The "Chock and Stir" method was a carefully devised way of taking hard ice cream and making it soft by me and my brother, Brett, in our younger years. This carefully thought out process involves taking your spoon and chopping your hard serve ice cream into smaller bits, and then giving it a good stir. Repeat the process a few times, and you have soft serve ice cream. Actually, many of us did or do something like this regularly. There is actually a reason, subconscious as it may be. It's easier to taste a warmer product.

You may say to yourself, why not just let it sit out for a few minutes? The answer to this is two fold. First, this method doesn't achieve the desired outcome. This method gives you a soupy ice cream, with hard ice cream left over. It's not evenly distributed. Secondly, it's ice cream, and waiting any longer than necessary just wasn't in the cards.

According to an infographic released at the end of 2016 by *Bundle*, a company which tracks money spending and saving trends, New Hampshirites eat more ice cream than most states. New Hampshire ranks as the 8th highest state when it comes to eating ice cream in the United States (I'm not including the highest "state" listed as Washington DC). In fact, four of the New England states, including Rhode Island, Connecticut, and Massachusetts, all finished in the top 10. Why do we love ice cream up here so much? One could easily assume the hottest states or the states with the longest summers would be the obvious choices here. Is it because we all love the cold so much that we've incorporated it into our diets?

I figured it was time to go on a mission, speak with the great people of the Granite State, and find out what they believe are the answers to these questions in the hopes that I'll find out something about our corner of the country, and perhaps something about myself. I love to bake, and there is something about homemade cookies that recipes don't include, but translate into the taste – and that's heart. I believe when you're creating something you want people to enjoy, you're putting a lot of heart into it. Why wouldn't ice cream be the same? Since I wanted to get to the heart of the matter, what better way to investigate than to travel the state to find homemade ice cream? So, that's what I did.

PARLORS

Growing up, we loved toppings on our ice cream. I still load up if I decide I'm going all out for my sugary confection that day. In many cases, Brett and I would find whatever toppings were even borderline acceptable to put on ice cream in the household. I'm certain that on more than one occasion our mother wasn't happy with her cake decorating crystals constantly being depleted.

Toppings on ice cream would continue to be a story generator as, on one occasion, we hit a local ice cream parlor on route 40 while riding in style in Mom's 1975 Cadillac, which she had just finished getting detailed. My brother got some kind of soft serve with rainbow sprinkles and managed to get more sprinkles all over the newly cleaned vehicle than he did in his mouth.

My recommendation? Get a bowl (and put the cone on top of the ice cream), you're less likely to lose melting ice cream that way as well.

Kellerhaus

LACONIA, NH

Kellerhaus opened up as a candy shop in 1906, originally in downtown Laconia. In the 1920s, they started making ice cream. In the 1960s, during a revitalization of downtown Laconia, the owner decided to look for other places to set up shop in the area. In 1966, they found the house in its current location. They make some great ice cream here, but what makes Kellerhaus different is the all-you-can-eat sundae bar. The topping bar has been a hit since its creation. First, you pay for your number of scoops for your "sundae," then you get your ice cream flavors, and then you get one pass through the toppings bar with anything and everything you want on the ice cream. It is not weighed, and some pass through with what looks like a pile of candy more than a sundae. This is a child's dream (and the dream of more than a few adults as well). Kellerhaus makes most of their own toppings including hot fudge, chocolate sauce, butterscotch, fruit, and marshmallow, among other things.

If you want to be the boring person who doesn't get the sundae, they'll give you free sprinkles on your ice cream. Current owners Daryl Dawson and Brian Head bought Kellerhaus in May 2017. All ice cream is made in-house except a few of their sorbets and sugar-free items. They serve mostly hard ice cream, but they do have a small selection of soft serve.

Laconia is a tourist destination, so they have a large retail area for visitors to the area with all kinds of things from clothing to trinkets. Though, the other main reason you would want to come to Kellerhaus is for the chocolates. Kellerhaus is a chocolatier and they have two machines dedicated to making the best milk and dark chocolates around. They make their own clusters, turtles, fudge, and I could keep listing all of the amazing chocolates they offer, but I can only fit so many words on the page... They have a candy smorgasbord for the kids to grab up a bunch of different candies sold by weight so variety can be an option. They do offer sugar-free chocolates, but they are normally brought in, not made on-site.

Daryl showed me their ice cream maker, remarking that, "we've been using this one since the 1920's." They have another one, but it's mainly "used for parts to keep this machine going." I've seen a lot of ice cream makers during the writing of this book, and they haven't changed too much since then. It takes the machine about ten minutes to make a batch, and they use a typical square box container to hold their ice cream to go into their batch freezer.

Daryl used to work with a biotech company, but he wanted to get into something different. The nostalgia of Kellerhaus is what really drew him into the idea of purchasing the business. He recounted a story of a woman who was in her 70s, who came in around Christmas time who told him about working in Kellerhaus when she was 16. That's the kind of history Kellerhaus has. Daryl believes that nostalgia, as well as the toppings bar, are what draws people back to Kellerhaus.

The most unique flavors they offer are cherry chocolate chip and black raspberry chip. They are looking to work on some new and unique flavors. They did a pumpkin pie last fall and that went over very well so they are going to look into putting some more seasonal flavors together. Vanilla is very popular (obviously for the sundaes) and the Cookie Monster is probably the most popular flavor outside of that. During the summer, they will go through 500-600 gallons of ice cream a week. Kellerhaus carries around 16 flavors, but the main attraction is the homemade toppings bar.

I spoke with customers Carol and Jack Dreyer while I was visiting. Carol had coffee ice cream and Jack went with coffee and

chocolate chip. Like me, Carol loves coffee ice cream, but not coffee. She says that the cream in the ice cream mostly eliminates the bitter elements of the coffee. They love bringing their grandchildren in to get the ice cream and hit the toppings bar. Carol helps out with the Moultonborough Library and she often makes raffle baskets around Halloween that include coffin shaped chocolates from Kellerhaus.

Daryl is from North Carolina originally and they have ice cream shops open year around, but here in New Hampshire, most ice cream shops don't stay open year around. He tends to believe that the reduced availability for an ice cream cone or sundae leads to the overwhelming excitement for ice cream when summer does finally arrive. However, it's worth noting that Kellerhaus is open all year long to satiate your needs. If you haven't made a trip for ice cream all winter long, you can harness that excitement and order The Colossus - a ten scoop bucket of amazingness which you can attempt to finish while your friends cheer you on (or more likely help you eat it). Kellerhaus will also ring a bell so that others can acknowledge your enthusiasm and bask in the glory of your courage.

Daryl and Brian love the creation of the chocolates and the ice cream. Their love for creating the products shines through on the customer's side as they've installed some chalkboards, welcoming customers to create as well. They have an indoor facility as well, so if it's raining, it's no big deal – or you can stop in and grab pints to take home. If you can't make it anytime soon, check out their website where you can order their chocolates. Sorry, you can't order ice cream to your doorstep yet, but you can purchase some from Ames Farms in Alton, and they are working on expanding distribution in the future.

Attractions in the area:

The lakes, plenty of hiking in the area, Funspot, Hart's Turkey Farm, Castle in the Clouds, Polar Caves, Gunstock Mountain Resort in the winter, ziplines in the summer/ropes courses

Visit Kellerhaus online at
www.kellerhaus.com
or they are located at
259 Endicott St N
Laconia, NH 03246

Walpole Creamery

WALPOLE, NH

Walpole Creamery was originally started by a couple of local gentlemen, but soon it got a bit too big for them, so another group of locals led by current majority owner Rob Kasper purchased it and hired Bobby Dorman to be the plant manager. Bobby has been in the food business for 25 years and previously owned a restaurant. In 2011, he attended the Penn State program. Rob is a 2014 graduate of the same program.

Walpole Creamery makes its own base mix on-site, which is not an easy undertaking. They get their raw milk from Crescent Farm, just three miles away, and then pasteurize and homogenize it themselves for use in the ice cream. The milk, cream, and milk powder are hormone free and antibiotic free, and their passion for keeping their ice cream all-natural shines through with every ingredient. The sugar used is a non-GMO cane sugar. Bobby believes people keep coming back because they make everything the old-fashioned way. They create a super-premium ice cream with a very low overrun. Walpole has a large focus on natural products and tries to source as locally as possible for their flavors. For example, their maple syrup comes from Twin Spruce Farm in Walpole. Walpole Creamery has been named "Best of NH" the past two years and its Real Maple Walnut was featured as one of the top flavors in New England in the June edition of *Yankee Magazine*.

The creamery puts out a lot of ice cream in the summer – as much as 6,000 pints of ice cream a week during the summer! They average about 3,000 pints of ice cream per week throughout the year but during the summer they sometimes have 13-hour work days because of the demand.

The more unique flavors are Fijan Ginger and Udder Joy (coconut, almonds, and chocolate chips). The coffee flavors, such as Mocha Chip, use freshly brewed coffee. The Strawberry Lemonade was a surprise find on the menu, and was every bit as refreshing as it sounds. The more popular flavors are

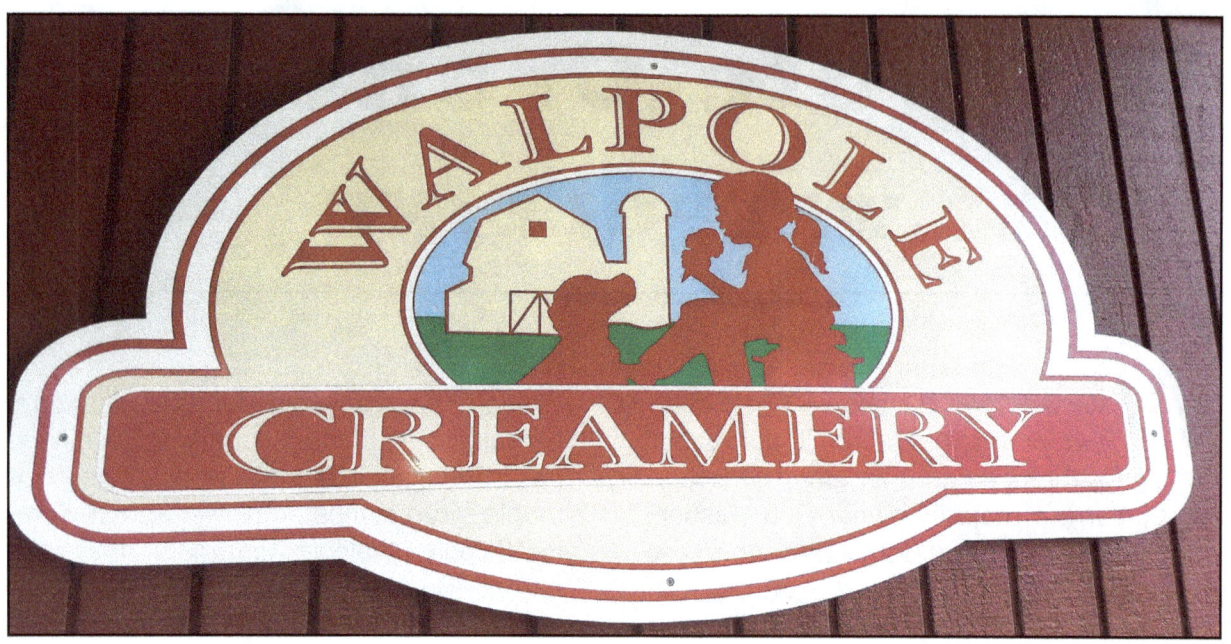

the Tahitian Vanilla and the Double Dutch Chocolate. I like my chocolate with a little bit more punch and the Double Dutch is an example of what lengths Walpole Creamery will go to create a quality product. In Double Dutch Chocolate, the cocoa is added to the cream and cooked right in at the beginning of the process, not added in with a cold base mix. Naturally, I like chocolate with my chocolate, so I opted for a scoop of Chocolate Indulgence which comes with chocolate crumbled sandwich cookies mixed into the Double Dutch, but I did offset that with a scoop of Mint Chip. I was joined on this trip by my friend Darryl who had the Maple Cream and the Caramel Cashew Chip flavors. If you're lucky enough to get here for the seasonal Coconut, give that a try. It was jam-packed with coconut sweetness and flakes. If you want to go completely over the top, try the Chocolate Triple Play, which is a combination of the chocolate, chocolate cookies, and chocolate chip cookie dough.

Bobby believes that for years New Hampshire has been one of the most popular destinations for ice cream as he's read about it in magazines over time. I suppose the quality of this ice cream combined with a desire to bring tourism into the state has done New Hampshire a deal of good when it comes to our favorite dessert. Walpole

Creamery ice cream is also available in over 220 grocery stores in NH, VT, and MA.

Bobby enjoys the people he works with at Walpole Creamery, it's probably the best part of his job. He tells me they've "all been there for seven or eight years and since everyone has a great handle on the job they get along well." In addition to that, they have a shop in Keene where Rob's wife, Barbara, makes the brownies and pastries from scratch for some of their menu choices. Enjoy a beautiful ride to the southwestern part of the state, stop in, and let me know - what's your favorite flavor?

Distribution:

Walpole Creamery has three different distributors: Associated Grocer, Sure Winner Foods run out of Saco, ME has their products in Hannaford, and Associated Buyers moves their product into Wholefoods, so you definitely have options if you can't make it to the Walpole shop.

Attractions in the area:

Walpole Mountain View Winery, Great River Outfitters, Downtown Keene for the other shop.

Visit Walpole Creamery online at
www.walpolecreamery.com
or they are located at
532 Main Street
Walpole, NH 03431

18 Degrees Celcius

NORTH CONWAY, NH

McKaella Schmitt previously owned a bakery in town, but then closed it to open an ice cream place about five years ago. She still bakes a few treats inside 18 Degrees Celcius, her micro batch ice cream parlor. McKaella went to culinary school in New York and worked at a few hotels before moving onto her solo projects. McKaella makes her own base mix on-site, and all of her flavors are made from scratch. She gets her cream from Hatchland Farms, and 18 Degrees Celcius also makes their own cones, and some of their toppings.

Some of the more unique flavors served are Honeycomb (it uses a honeycomb looking brittle like candy), Green Tea, Lemon Gingersnap, Lavender with White Chocolate, and the Avalanche which is a chocolate base flavor that incorporates their "Avalanche brownies." The brownies are made from chocolate, peanut butter, marshmallow and Rice Krispies. I saw them in front of me and thought I'd be leaving with one until I found out they were used in the ice cream. From there it was a foregone conclusion that I was walking away with a scoop of that. Olivia, McKaella's daughter, who was setting up shop like a seasoned professional while I was doing this interview (she couldn't have barely been double digits in age) threw out her own suggestion of the Unicorn Chaser which is a rainbow cake flavored ice cream. The Green Tea is interesting in that it has a unique shade of green which children sometimes want to try, and then usually, and surprisingly, enjoy, despite the unexpected taste.

The most popular flavors at 18 Degrees Celcius are the Vanilla, Chocolate, Chocolate Chip and Pineapple Peach. They rotate many of their flavors, so apart from the Salted Caramel, Vanilla, Chocolate, and Coffee, the flavor you're eyeing may not be there next week, so take the chance. Some of these selections are too unique to pass on. If you're a pistachio fan, this is a great stop for you as well. It's easy to see why the

Salted Caramel is always on this list. It's such a bold flavor and McKaella jokes that she's made it a bit too dark on more than one occasion.

One thing that clearly sets 18 Degrees apart from other ice cream shops in the area is something you aren't likely to find anywhere else in the state. Their donut ice cream sandwiches are a signature item, and yes, they make the donuts themselves as well. Not feeling ice cream, but still seeking something cold? Give their homemade popsicles a try, which kind of take the place of a sorbet option here due to the limited space in the shop. They have mostly fruit flavored popsicles, but they do have one that is a cereal popsicle which contains Fruity Pebbles.

It doesn't end there. They also make frappes and floats including a Moxie float if that happens to be your thing. They also have gluten free & vegan ice creams as well as ice cream sandwiches. 18 Degrees Celcius is generally open by late May and they tend to stay open a little later than some shops, usually into November.

It's clear that McKaella's work ethic and joyful demeanor has rubbed off on her daughter; but it helps to be in the business of making people happy. McKaella says she tries "to keep it super basic, super simple, clean, no additives, and [she doesn't] like using corn syrup." It makes sense as a micro-batch ice cream maker; any small thing at that level can change the taste in drastic fashion, so attention to detail is a must. Here at 18 Degrees Celcius, no detail is spared, and you'll be walking away knowing you made a wise decision to stop here for your ice cream.

Distribution:

The Vista, The White Mountain Cider Co. Deli, Tamworth Lyceum, Huttopia, Boston Brothers Pizzeria

Attractions in the area:

Conway Scenic Railroad, Mount Washington attractions, hiking, pretty much everything, honestly if you can't find something to do in or around Conway, you're not looking...

Visit 18 Degrees Celsius at
2683 White Mountain Highway
North Conway, NH 03860

Moo's Place

DERRY, NH

Moo's Place has been around for fourteen years in its Derry location and seven years ago they opened a parlor in Salem. Steve and Christy LaRocca were both in the airline industry and did a lot of traveling to the UK since Steve has family there. They originally wanted to open a tea shop but realized the demographics weren't right for the business. Christy came across a flyer for an ice cream place that happened to be for sale and together they thought that Derry could use an ice cream parlor. Moo's Place generally opens from April 1st through Columbus Day.

Moo's Place does make a few of their flavors and Steve is proud of some of their fall seasonal flavors such as their apple crisp and the berry cobbler. They also make their own cheesecake flavor. Moo's uses a 14% butterfat mix. They shop around for the other flavors they use as they're particular about what they add to their ice cream. They get peaches and apples from the Hazelton Farm in Chester that they use for their fall seasonal flavors. They make their own brownies and cookies as well, but they're known for their seasonal assortment of flavors which uses these local products. Moo's place has a very nice indoor atmosphere with seating, which offers some respite from the heat or rain depending on the day, yet they still maintain windows for outside customers.

Steve says they run on the principles of "good ice cream, great service, and a clean environment, [and] that's what we strive for." Steve and Christy's lives revolve around the parlor, and they want to create a strong tradition that will be passed on to someone else in the future. Their most popular flavor is the Cookie Dough – and it rivals their Vanilla in sales which is saying a lot considering the lineup of sundaes they offer at Moo's. Mint Chip and Black Raspberry come close, but the Cookie Dough reigns supreme here. Steve made me up a sampler which included the Cookie Dough, Cheesecake, Mint Oreo and the Frozen Pudding, a unique flavor popular many years ago which is essentially a fruitcake ice cream – and it's well worth the visit. The Double Chocolate Brownie isn't to be missed either.

Moo's makes their own ice cream cakes as well, and they're pretty popular. I was there just after Mother's Day and Steve told me that between the two stores, they sold over seventy-five cakes in that time period. Steve enjoys hearing the feedback and comments from people who love and appreciate the service they get from their staff. One of his favorite things about the parlor is working with the kids they employ since they help to maintain a light and fun atmosphere. He also remarked on his repeat customers and how happy they are coming to the shop. Moo's contributes a lot to their surrounding community, going as far as putting a form on their website for those who are fundraising in the area to request donations. Steve remarked that even his employees get in on the action by donating all of the pennies they receive throughout the year in their tips to good causes; he noted that they donated around $2,000 dollars between Make a Wish and a local SPCA.

Moo's also makes hard serve yogurts and Italian water ice. They make their own cookies and brownies for the sundaes. In addition to that, they cater and make use of an ice cream cart with an umbrella at events. Also, if you're in a hurry or don't want to eat your ice cream there, they do have some flavors available for purchase in half gallon tubs. Moo's is a pretty nice spot and offers a good variety of everything and falls in line with what someone should expect from an ice cream parlor. The Salem shop has an antique/vintage car evening once a week with music which can make for a nice, inexpensive family outing.

Attractions in the area:

Robert Frost house, Manchester is nearby.

Visit Moo's Place online at
www.moosplace.com
or they are located at
27 Crystal Avenue
Derry, NH 03038

Beyond Vanilla

HAMPSTEAD, NH

Paul Antosh originally hails from Texas and always enjoyed cooking and barbecuing. He had the idea for an ice cream shop after helping some friends start up a restaurant. Paul thought it would be a fun project to start with his children and has been making ice cream since 2005. In March 2016, he purchased their current location which was originally called Flying Cow and renamed the store Beyond Vanilla.

Paul was working with a baker who made everything from scratch, and not all bakers do that. Paul realized that making his ice cream with the utmost quality would involve making everything from scratch as well, and by everything, he meant his flavors. Beyond Vanilla makes their ice cream five gallons at a time. According to Paul, "The advantage of doing five gallons at a time is that there is more control over the ingredients."

Paul says, "Chocolate ice cream is like wine." He starts his chocolate from a high-quality cocoa powder and sugar. Even Paul's brownies start with pounds of dark chocolate, as he makes those from scratch as well for their sundaes. Many people claim they are the best brownies they've ever had. It's this dedication to a quality product that brings people back to Beyond Vanilla.

The focus of Beyond Vanilla tends to be a three-pronged approach that involves coffee-based ice creams, ice creams that use alcohol, and vegan/sugar-free/dairy-free ice cream options. This isn't just a casual walk down each path; Paul actively seeks out ways for each of these directions to improve upon his creations. Beyond Vanilla currently has three Coffee flavors, Columbia Coffee which is their basic dark roast coffee, Coffee Oreo, and Cowboy Coffee Cookie Dough. Cowboy Coffee Cookie Dough is the signature flavor of Beyond Vanilla and it's one of the major reasons that people come back.

If alcohol in your ice cream is something

that you love – or something you haven't tried, you may never want to venture far from Beyond Vanilla. They have quite a few options in store for you. Paul says that most of his adult customers have switched from the Vanilla flavor to his Cognac Vanilla; it offers that extra something on late summer nights. For Beyond Vanilla's Rum Raisin Ice Cream, he notes that rum, like all alcohol, is sugar and always being wary of making his ice creams too sweet, Paul decided that instead of trying to mix in the rum with his ice cream that a better move would be to soak the raisins in rum. Instead of an overly sweet ice cream, the experience leads to small bursts of rum flavor when eating the raisins. By far the biggest standout among the alcohol ice creams is his Bourbon Chocolate. Paul almost doesn't even want to put the word chocolate out there for the chocolate lovers as the flavor really is bourbon. You'll be hard-pressed to find such a strong and unique flavor combination that uses bourbon in the world of ice cream.

Beyond Vanilla also has a lot of vegan, dairy-free and sugar-free options. Vegan Chocolate Coconut is a very dark chocolate and you don't need to be vegan to enjoy it. There is so much flavor in this that you just don't expect when it comes to a vegan option. Paul's big on not using more sugar than necessary. When it comes to sugar-free options, he works with a company called Luv who shares a goal of bringing in more flavor while finding ways to reduce sugar without sacrificing taste.

If you're looking for something a bit different, try the Bananas Foster Frappe which incorporates rum, butter, and brown sugar and of course, bananas. The Dulce de Leche is mixed with a pound cake and is one of the more unique offerings at Beyond Vanilla. Beyond Vanilla makes their own slushies as well. After my visit, it was obvious that Paul and his staff take a lot of pride and put a lot of hard work into creating their unique and powerful flavors. Schedule a trip this summer so you don't miss out on a true gem among ice cream parlors in New Hampshire.

Attractions in the area:

Great trails to walk, Sweet Baby Vineyard (tours & tastings), Honey Bee Haven (antique shop), there are summer concerts by the Civic Club.

Visit Beyond Vanilla at
16 Main Street
Hampstead, NH 03841

- RASPBERRY TRUFFLE
- PEPPERMINT STICK
- BUTTERCRUNCH
- COCONUT CREAM
- PISTACHIO
- REVERSE CHIP
- SALTED CARAMEL COOKIES & CREAM
- MAPLE WALNUT
- SWEET CREAM & BROWNIES
- Key Lime Pie
- COTTON CANDY
- HEATH BAR
- COOKIES & CREAM
- ORANGE SHERBET
- LEMON SORBET

LOW FAT FROZEN YOGURT

- TRIPLE CHOCOLATE
- CHOC. PEANUT BUTTER CUP
- MINT CHIP
- BLACK RASPBERRY

Jordan's Ice Creamery

BELMONT, NH

Jordan's Ice Creamery was started by Eric Jordan in 1996. He was a school teacher and he wanted to continue teaching children but earn some extra income during the summer. He originally owned Belmont Village Store which was a small convenience store in downtown Belmont. Upon purchasing that, the sale came with the current spot of land where Jordan's Homemade Ice Cream is located today. Eric passed ownership over to his son Craig and they've opened a second location near Funspot in Laconia, NH.

I spoke with Brad Reep, one of the managers at Jordan's, and he told me that "cleanliness, great staff, and a great product are what leads to a successful ice cream parlor and repeat customers." Some of the more unique flavors offered at Jordan's are the Salted Caramel Cookies and Cream and the Raspberry Cheesecake. A few years ago, Jordan's started a program of rotating in new flavors for a one-month limited time period. These temporary ice cream flavors come served as a flight on a board (think beer tastings, but ice cream instead) and you receive four flavors in sampler size dishes.

The most popular flavors at Jordan's are Raspberry Truffle, Cookie Dough, Coconut Cream, and Moose Tracks. They even offer a Banana ice cream, and the followers of Jordan's (they have over 10,000 on Facebook) are very loyal to their particular flavors.

When Jordan's first opened, they started on Mother's Day, and now they are opening as early as March 9th and customers are still showing up in their coats to get their favorite ice creams. They make their own sorbets and sherbets as well, though they do try to hold off on those until later in the year for higher temperatures. They make frozen yogurt as well and some of their most popular flavors are Black Raspberry Chocolate Chip and the Chocolate Peanut

Butter Cup. They have a soft-serve frozen yogurt as well including a Maple, Black Raspberry, and Coffee Kahlua. Later in the season, they will have a Pineapple for the hot days. Jordan's signature item is the Belly Buster, which is five scoops in a pail which comes with hot fudge, whipped cream, nuts, a banana, and a cookie.

Jordan's is in a location that is great for repeat business; many of the people who come by are locals and have a regular order that they get every day or once a week. The staff really love the amount of local support they get at this shop. Jordan's has won best of New Hampshire and has also placed high on the yearly WMUR poll. They make their own cookies and waffle cones as well as a continued quest to maintain a high-quality product.

Brad's favorite thing about working at Jordan's is getting in the new hires, the next generation of kids who they teach and grow over a few years to become better in the job as well as life. Brad has been here himself for twelve years, started as a junior in high school, and learned firsthand the knowledge he is now passing on to the new staff.

I took it as a sign when the two people in front of me had the Sweet Cream and Brownies with the Salted Caramel Cookies and Cream. After seeing two orders of these go one right after the other, I figured they were popular for a reason so I ordered scoops of those plus a scoop of Key Lime Pie and I wasn't disappointed, and nor will you be if you can make it out to Jordan's.

Distribution :

Jordan's does distribute to a few local places. Keens and Greens in Gilford, Osborne Agways, Tilton, Concord and Hooksett, Case and Keg in Laconia and Meredith. They sell packaged ice cream. There is a place in Meredith that scoops Jordan's ice cream, but they are particular on who scoops their ice cream as they have their name attached and want to make sure that the ice cream is preserved and kept properly.

Attractions in the area:

Gale school, Mount Major is in Gilford, one of the largest vendors at the speedway. Belknap Mountain in Gilford.

Visit Jordan's Ice Creamery at
894 Laconia Road
Belmont, NH 03220

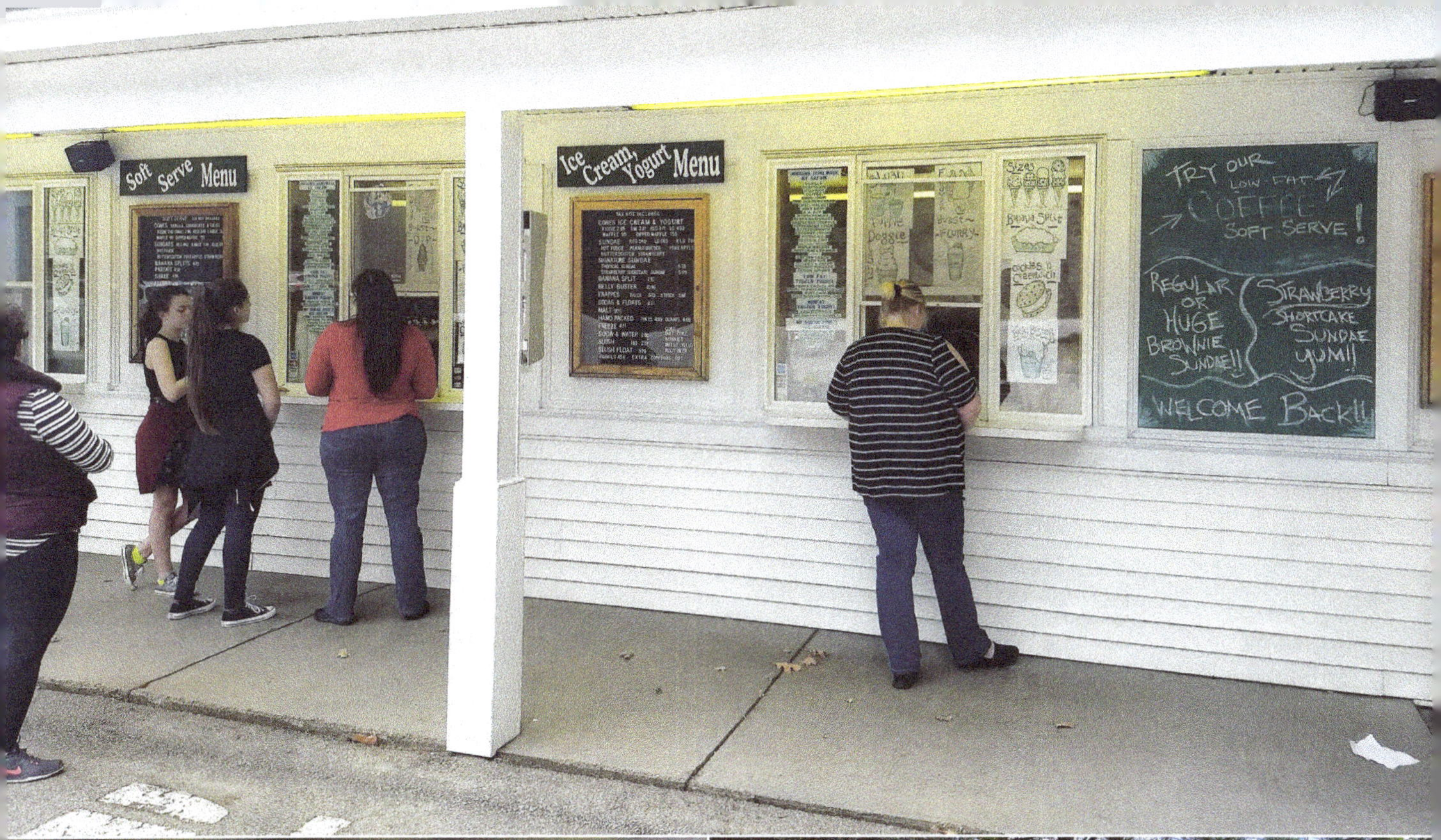

CREMELAND

~FLAVORS~

HARD SERVE: (Made here at Cremeland)
- Vanilla
- Chocolate
- Strawberry
- Coffee
- Black Raspberry
- Pistachio
- Chocolate Chip
- Mint Chip
- Cherry Vanilla
- Butter Pecan
- Oreo
- Birthday Cake
- Piña Colada
- Banana
- Bubblegum
- M+M
- Chocolate Walnut
- Red Raspberry
- Orange Freeze
- Peanut Butter
- Turtle
- Cookie Dough

Cookie Monster

SOFT SERVE:
- Chocolate
- Vanilla
- Sour Power Kids

FROZEN YOGURT:
- Mocha Toffee Chunk

SHERBET:
- Orange

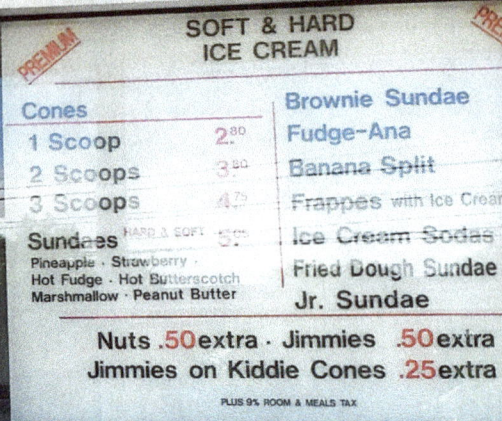

SOFT & HARD ICE CREAM

Cones	
1 Scoop	2.80
2 Scoops	3.80
3 Scoops	4.70

Sundaes HARD & SOFT
Pineapple · Strawberry
Hot Fudge · Hot Butterscotch
Marshmallow · Peanut Butter

- Brownie Sundae
- Fudge-Ana
- Banana Split
- Frappes with Ice Cream
- Ice Cream Sodas
- Fried Dough Sundae
- Jr. Sundae

Nuts .50 extra · Jimmies .50 extra
Jimmies on Kiddie Cones .25 extra

PLUS 9% ROOM & MEALS TAX

ICE CREAM SANDWICHES
Chocolate or Vanilla
EACH $1.45 or 6 PACK $7.25
PLUS TAX

There is a $10.00 minimum for the use of charge cards.

No public restrooms

COTTON CANDY $2.50
HOMEMADE

There is $10.00 minimum for use of CARDS

No Soliciting

Cremeland Drive In
MANCHESTER, NH

Nicole Queena is a third-generation owner of the Cremeland Drive In. It's been in the family for over seventy-five years and she's been there since she was ten years old. She started managing when she was seventeen. Nicole will be the first to tell you that the business is tough to run, and she puts in a lot of hours. She was told by her parents that she needed to go to college or run the restaurant. She didn't care for school, so she made the decision rather quickly. It was obviously the right decision as she loves the business and the work.

The first thing that you'll find out about Cremeland is it's more than an ice cream shop. They make fresh seafood here – nothing is frozen. They make their own coleslaw, chili, and sauces as well. So, if you decide to come with an appetite, you'll easily be satiated. Cremeland is known for their fried clams, so if you're coming for the seafood and are hit with indecisiveness, go for those. They are constantly adding and changing menu items, so it's worth checking in periodically to see what's new.

When I arrived Nicole was talking about one of her new flavors in which she's still working on improving, a Sour Power Kids, which is a sour base with sour patch kids in it. Nicole seems to have adjusted well to the ever-changing trends that come with what children want in their ice cream. Cremeland is starting to work with cotton candy. They sell actual cotton candy as well as work with a cotton candy ice cream base. If this sounds like it would be up your alley, have a Cotton Candy Burrito Sundae.

The best seller here is the Cookie Monster, which has a blue cotton candy base, Oreos, and cookie dough pieces. Nicole never expected this flavor to end up being one of the most popular. She was even surprised one day when her dentist remarked about how great the flavor was, not realizing he was speaking to the owner. While they have a hard time keeping up with the demand for the Cookie Monster, Vanilla and Chocolate are unsurprisingly leading sellers.

Some of the more unique flavors you'll find at Cremeland are their Blueberry Cheesecake and their Espresso Toffee Fudge. The Espresso Toffee Fudge is not a vanilla base ice cream with espresso pieces, but instead, the base itself is espresso flavored. If fruit flavors are your thing, they have Banana, Strawberry Mango and the Very Berry Blueberry. I enjoyed a combo of the Very Berry Blueberry and the Raspberry Chocolate Chip on a second trip back. It was refreshing on what was a very hot day.

Cremeland has a different atmosphere about it. Since it's a drive-in, people will sit in their cars to eat and there are benches outside as well. It's laid back in such a way that even some people tailgate with their dogs and talk to the other customers after they grab up their food from the windows, giving it a nice social vibe. Speaking of dogs, they do have doggy ice cream sandwiches for the overheated puppies. On the same topic, their hot dogs have won awards.

Nostalgia is one of the big reasons people come back to Cremeland, people whose parents brought them there as children come back later in life. Nicole's favorite thing about working at the ice cream stand is getting to work with the kids.

"I love working with the kids," she said. "I love them, they're like my family, some of them have been with me for thirty years. The most enjoyable thing is to see them develop and mature."

She likes to see them become stronger with interpersonal skills and grow into young adults before they go on to other things in life. Cremeland tends to open in early March until the end of October. Nicole does what she can to help support community events and sports, so consider returning the love by stopping here on a hot day.

Attractions in the area:

Northeast Delta Dental Stadium to see the Fishercats baseball team, Currier Museum of Art.

Visit Cremeland Drive In at
250 Valley Road
Manchester, NH 03103

Bishop's Homemade Ice Cream

LITTLETON, NH

Opening in 1976, Bishop's Homemade Ice Cream is one of the more well-known and quantifiable staples of the North Country's dessert options. Under new ownership recently, Steve and Kasie Pilgrim have teamed up with Dan and Jade Walker to continue bringing the same quality of New Hampshire's favorite treat. All four grew up in Littleton. In fact, Dan grew up three doors down from the shop, and Jade's first work outside the family business was scooping ice cream at Bishop's. All four of the owners have full-time work elsewhere; but Dan and Steve own a trucking company together, so they already had some experience working together.

The original owners, Race and Bill Bishop, operated Bishop's for about fifteen years. It's changed hands a few times since then, but when the opportunity came to purchase, the four seized the chance since there were some concerns that someone may purchase the property for real estate, but not renew the business, and Bishop's was too important to them and the rest of the community. Bishop's makes their ice cream with a 14% butterfat base mix and tends to keep around 16-20 flavors. This depends on both a rotating schedule as well as seasonal options. In a short time, they've already been commissioned to do a custom flavor for an anniversary, and have had a school class make their own flavors as well. So, keep in mind that they're always looking for inspiration from the community.

Their signature flavor is the Bishop's Bash. It's a much darker, richer base than their usual chocolate, and includes brownies, walnuts, and chocolate chunks. The most popular flavors are Mocha Cookies and Cream and the Black Raspberry, a traditional hit in the granite state. I found myself enjoying the Irish Cream. The Pecan Praline was refreshing, and I was happy and surprised to find a Creamy Lemon

flavor as that's generally a flavor reserved for sorbet. The Reese's Pieces flavor is an excellent choice, especially if you're a chocolate lover, as this usually is a flavor reserved for a vanilla base, not chocolate.

Even though they're new to ice cream ownership, they're clearly learning quickly. Dan told me "you learn a lot about what works and what doesn't when it comes to mixing the ice cream." I myself would be doing way more "testing" than need be. The nostalgia of the place is a big draw for Bishop's. Jade said, "Our children are 4th generation customers." She spoke to a gentleman during a soft opening of the store for the season and he was from Ohio, but originally from this area. He said that he had to bring his family here – and that's a common thing, people always want to come back. Bishop's has a nice family atmosphere and their commitment to the community makes this establishment feel open and welcoming.

Bishop's doesn't just make their own ice cream, they make their own cookies for their cookie sandwiches, and they make cakes and pies as well. They also make their own whoopie pies for their whoopie pie sundaes. In addition to that, they make their own waffle cones and bowls. If you're looking for some options other than ice cream, they do make their own frozen yogurts and sorbets, and also have a soft serve for those who don't want hard serve. Bishop's is currently seasonal and they generally open in April.

Jade loves working in the ice cream shop because everyone loves ice cream and with a smaller community, you see many friends and family. They believe they stand out from other places in the area as their indoor facility is family friendly and their ice cream is high quality – and I might add, allows you to enjoy ice cream even during a thunderstorm. Traveling with a four-legged friend? They have pup cups and water bowls for the members of your family who

are canine. So, plan a trip to this beautiful town, but also come for the Bishop's Bash, because while Bishop's does distribute, you can only find this flavor at the scoop shop.

Distribution:

Bishop's distributes to AMC Highland Center and The Littleton Co-op. They are open to creating custom flavors for restaurants or stores. Please note that the Bishop's Bash is only available at the scoop shop.

Attractions in the area:

Antiquing, Shilling Beer Company, which has a covered bridge right near it, and Chutters Candy Shop.

Visit Bishop's Homemade Ice Cream online at
www.bishopshomemadeicecream.com
or they are located at
183 Cottage Street
Littleton, NH 03561

Memories Ice Cream

KINGSTON, NH

Memories Ice Cream used to be a dairy farm which housed over 300 cows. The land started to be sold off a few decades ago until eventually the cows were gone, and in 1993 the property was turned into an ice cream stand. Five years ago, Steve Padfield purchased the place.

Steve Padfield was in the gas station and convenience store business for thirty-five years, but he started growing a bit tired of the 24/7 work life. He sold Memories Ice Cream at one of his convenience store locations and noticed that it was selling very well. In a conversation one day with the prior owner, he asked to be notified if the business ever went up for sale. Months later, he received that phone call and is clearly happy with his decision to purchase Memories Ice Cream.

Memories Ice Cream still distributes their ice cream. When Steve bought the place, they only sold at two locations, but they now sell at over ten locations and they reach as far as Concord. They sell to a few restaurants and country stores as well.

Memories Ice Cream makes about half of their own bases, and have numerous flavors only found here. They have a couple of organic ice creams they make on their own as well and they're also working on a "nice cream" which is a vegan take on ice cream.

The country setting with the barn, silo, and the goats are a big attraction for those looking to come out for ice cream on a nice warm day. It's also a beautiful back route for motorcycles and vacationers during the summer season. While the cows are no longer there, the dairy spirit lives on. Vanilla is the most popular flavor because of all the sundaes and frappes offered at Memories, though Mint Chocolate Chip is probably the next best seller.

Memories Ice Cream is known for their unique flavors which include but aren't

limited to - Beet & Goat Cheese (yes, you heard that right), Cabernet Crunch (thirty bottles of wine simmered down and added to their ice cream mix with chocolate chips thrown in for good measure), and Ginger Mascarpone, which is one of their most popular flavors. The process involves peeling ginger root, candying it and mixing that with mascarpone cheese. They also make a Honey Lavender with honey from their own bees and a helpful neighbor. If you like spicy things, try the Fireball flavor which is a cinnamon and hot pepper ice cream. Just about any flavor you can think of is made here, and undoubtedly, many flavors you'd never have thought of being here as well. Other flavors I sampled included the Maple Bourbon, Cherry Chip, Red Raspberry Chip, a Strawberry Thyme Sorbet, Chocolate Walnut, and of course, a Double Chocolate Brownie Batter.

Steve thinks that New Hampshirites secretly love the cold and noted a few days when they first opened for the season where customers were wearing their winter coats but still wanted their ice cream. A makeshift enclosure is added to the farmers porch in the early spring and late fall to make it a little warmer. Coconut Chip is the signature flavor and it's one of the reasons he bought the place. Indian Pudding is one flavor that is very difficult to find anymore, but they also make this – from scratch!

One of the highlights of the job for Steve is making new flavors and the creative process involved with that, and the menu clearly shows this, offering many flavors that I've never seen. Steve's son Alex makes much of the ice cream and enjoys working there during the summer months so he can head southwest for hiking and rock climbing during the winter.

Steve says, "One of the things we pride ourselves on is the amount of things we use from our little property here," which is about three acres. They have their own apple trees, peach trees, blueberry bushes, honey, and maple trees, which they use for some of their flavors. Many years ago, the barn was used to sell baked goods and other products. Steve says that there are plans in the works to open the barn up once again.

Memories Ice Cream makes their own ice cream cakes, sorbets, sherbets, and waffle cones. They also make homemade cookies, which are used for their ice cream sandwiches, which have become a very popular item. You'd be doing yourself a disservice by not stopping here while you're in the area and trying something you're not likely to find anywhere else.

DISTRIBUTION:

Farmstands & Country Stores:

The Farm at Eastman's Corner Kensington NH, Calef Country Store Barrington, NH, Moulton's Market Amherst, NH, Newfields Country Store Newfields, NH, Hampstead Center Market Hampstead, NH, LaValley Farms Hooksett, NH, True Confections Candy & Gifts Concord, NH

Scoop Shops:

The Creamery. Applecrest Farms Hampton Falls, NH, Triple Elm Coffee & Ice Cream Sandown, NH

Restaurants:

Epoch at the Exeter Inn Exeter, NH, Blue Moon Evolution Exeter, NH

ATTRACTIONS IN THE AREA:

Kingston Lake for fishing, boating, and swimming, Applecrest Orchards (which is one of their customers).

Visit Memories Ice Cream online at
www.memoriesicecream.com
or they are located at
95 Exeter Road
Kingston, NH 03848

Hayward's Ice Cream
NASHUA, NH

Hayward's is one of the most well-known ice cream parlors in the state, and there is a good reason. Hayward's opened their shop in 1940 and their strong ties to the community combined with their longevity, quality product, and the influx of Massachusetts residents coming across the border help keep this establishment as one of the top producers in the state – selling around 30,000 gallons of ice cream in a season. On an average day, they can go through around 125 gallons of ice cream; but on a busy day, they can sell anywhere from 200-250 gallons of ice cream, making them the largest volume seller in the state.

Anyone that knows me, knows I'm a chocoholic, but the most popular flavor at Hayward's is actually their vanilla. Owner Chris Ordway spoke to that quality when he told me the costs associated with their high-quality vanilla extract, and a 16% butterfat mix. Chris is a third generation Hayward, who started helping out at the shop in 1990 and eventually took it over from his father in 1996. Chris' grandparents started this adventure as an extension for their dairy farm in Milford but looked for another location since his grandfather's brother had an ice cream stand just down the road from their farm, Nashua ended up being the benefactor. Chris said, "You can still taste the vanilla after you're done eating it," so I sampled some, and this proved to be true. There was no hesitation from him that this was by far the most popular flavor. This was even more impressive considering my palette was probably altered after sampling the Chocolate Tsunami, by far the most chocolate of their ice creams including a chocolate base, chocolate chips, and brownies with chocolate chips in them.

Hayward's has eleven windows on three sides of their building for customers flocking in during the summer and Chris believes one of the reasons they keep coming back is their constant pursuit of the best ingredients, including their toppings. Some of their most unique flavors include Polar Cave (a vanilla with fudge swirls and caramel filled truffles), Kangamangus (a vanilla with a caramel swirl and chocolate covered pretzels – and yes, this is an intentional misspelling), and the Appalachian Trail (an espresso ice cream with a thick fudge swirl and heath bar candy pieces).

As we talked about the love people have for ice cream, Chris pointed out that "it's likely we eat so much more in New England because hard scoop ice cream places are more of a Northeast region thing." Some places are just too hot to have it and it would melt too quickly unless inside facilities were available. Many places only have soft serve as an option in the south and west. Something you're unlikely to find outside of Hayward's is a double stuffed Oreo, double stuffed coffee Oreo and what they've dubbed, the Black Diamond. They use the cream from the Oreo before it's hardened as part of their mix for these three flavors. The Oreo ice cream bases used for these flavors have chunks of the Oreo cream in it as well. Black Diamond is a chocolate ice cream with cookie dough pieces in addition to the Oreo cream mix.

One luxury that Hayward's staff has is that they have two ice cream makers, allowing

them to have fun with some of their flavors. The staff can have a brownie base ice cream started in one maker, and a cookie dough ice cream started in the other. Every inch or two they switch the buckets to create a layered effect for their Cookie Dough Brownie flavor. They repeat this process for a few other flavors.

Hayward's sells by the scoop, so you define what your own large ice cream is because you pick the number of scoops and you can mix them with no problems. After five or six scoops, they recommend putting your ice cream into a container. Chris remarked on a 60-scoop bowl they did for the mayor of Nashua, which was done in the style of a color wheel. Their homemade prowess isn't confined to just ice cream, however, as I observed them making their own sorbet. In addition to that, they make their own waffle cones and whipped cream, which adds an additional touch of freshness.

Places in the area to visit:

30 minutes from Boston, 20 minutes from Mount Monadnock. Nashua is known for its restaurants. They have more restaurants than any other city in NH. Pheasant Lane Mall, Nashua music festival (three during the year), a town holiday stroll, Greeley Park with state, kid events.

Visit Hayward's Ice Cream online at
www.haywardsicecream.com
or they are located at
7 Daniel Webster Highway
Nashua, NH 03060

Bruster's Ice Cream
NASHUA, NH

Bruster's is a franchise, but DO NOT let that fool you. Local owners Dawn and Bill Croteau opened up their shop in 2002 and pride themselves on providing the freshest ice cream with the highest quality ingredients. They are the only Bruster's in New England and owe their staying power in a state overwhelmed with ice cream parlors to their quality and commitment. When they first opened, they had a stand-alone building with walk-up windows, from 2002-2015. They decided with that business model allowing ice cream service for only eight months or so during the year, that they needed a change. That change came in the form of a new property with an indoor facility. This allows for business not only during the winter months but also during those rainy spring and summer days.

Bill used to be an engineer, Dawn used to be a travel agent. They did well in their professions, but decided they wanted to do something together that would be fun. They don't like anything that is average, but because they make the ice cream fresh in the store every day, they decide what flavors they want to make, they keep the quality high, and they also seek out the highest quality product they can find for their mix-ins and toppings. Bill said upon visiting another establishment years back that it "drives me crazy when I order a chocolate peanut butter cup ice cream and there are only two pieces of peanut butter cup in the ice cream," and he took these things to heart when they opened Bruster's and made sure that their "ice cream is loaded with all kinds of the extras and it's high quality."

Bruster's Ice Cream has their own dairy farm in Pennsylvania where the mix is produced to supply the ice cream shop. They talked to me about the ice cream needing to be tempered at many places where it comes out of the machine very

61

Key Lime Pie is one of their more unique flavors, and when it was first introduced, the plan was to only offer it during the summer. When it was removed from the menu in the fall, so many customers voiced their displeasure that they had to bring it back. It's been on the menu ever since and when you have some, you'll know why. It was late in life when I finally decided to give the Key Lime Pie a chance. I've only had this flavor of ice cream once or twice in my life, so you don't miss these opportunities when presented to you. It was as amazing as you should expect a key lime pie ice cream to be. It was the perfect amount of tangy-ness and graham cracker flavor sweetness to end a meal (or start one as I've been known to do).

Bruster's has two unique turtle flavors. They have a chocolate or vanilla base with caramel and pecans. Now when they use pecans, they actual put pecans in the ice cream, not little tiny bits of what once may have been pecans. In fact, one of the boxes of mix-ins Bill showed me during my visit was an entire box of whole pecans and I had to resist the urge to dive in. I thought to myself that Mom would be jealous of this trip as she's always had a love of pecans and passed that trait on to me.

Some of their most popular flavors include soft and then needs to be frozen and then pulled out later for serving. Bruster's prides themselves on being able to serve the ice cream immediately out of the machine. The process Bruster's uses involves whipping less air into the ice cream, giving it a creamier taste. They actually make their ice cream in two gelato machines to assist with keeping the ice cream denser. In addition to their fresh ice cream, they also hand make their waffle cones every day in the store.

62

Mint Chocolate Chip, Oreo, Chocolate Raspberry Truffle which is chocolate ice cream with a black raspberry ripple and chocolate flakes (and I highly recommend it). I'm in a constant battle with my father over the use of chocolate when combined with raspberry. He doesn't believe they belong together; whereas, I believe taking two awesome things like this and combining them, makes it more awesome-er. In addition to this, their Sea Salt Caramel, all of their coconut flavors, and peanut butter flavors (5 or more flavors, rotating periodically) sell well.

Bill believes that the popularity of ice cream in New Hampshire is based upon the rich dairy heritage of the New England states. For those who are interested, Bill and Dawn also run a concession trailer that they take to different fairs, events, and other happenings throughout the Northeast.

Attractions in the area:

Anheuser-Busch Brewery in Merrimack to see the Clydesdales, the Merrimack outlets.

Visit Bruster's online at
www.brustersexpress.com/nashua
or they are located at
621 Amherst Street
Nashua, NH 03063

Ilsley's Ice Cream

WEARE, NH

Lisa Ilsley is a fifth-generation dairy farmer, and fourth-generation at Ilsley's current location in Weare. They have eighteen milking cows on the farm. Lisa has future plans to get pasteurization equipment so Ilsley's can use their own cream base mix and make everything there on site. After graduating from UNH, Lisa purchased Brick Farm Ice Cream out of Unity, New Hampshire, moved it to Weare, and in 2014, Ilsley's opened up. Originally, Lisa's plan was to make cheese as she was looking for something that added value to the milking cows. Instead, the ice cream business just kind of fell into her lap and seemed like an obvious natural fit so she rolled with it. Ilsley's uses as many natural flavors as possible, including fruit purees and cocoa powder; however, you're more than welcome to toss gummy bears, Oreos, and assorted candies on top of your natural strawberry ice cream.

Brown Sugar Oatmeal is easily the most unique flavor and their bestseller. This is essentially their signature item and I haven't seen this flavor anywhere else nor have I tasted anything quite like it. Carrot Cake ice cream is also a unique flavor – one I've found at only a few other locations; though it doesn't have the chunks of cake in it, the flavor has all the spices that the carrot cake does, the same goes for the German Chocolate Cake. Flavors are rotated often here as she can only keep about fifteen flavors on the menu, including sorbets, at one time due to the smaller size of the parlor. Gold Rush is an interesting flavor as customers inquired about cookie dough in a chocolate base as opposed to vanilla, so Lisa did that with a caramel swirl.

Some of the more popular flavors are the Raspberry Chocolate Chunk, which is made with a red, not black, raspberry, Maple Cream which uses their Sweet Cream ice cream base and added maple syrup (note this does not have walnuts in it) and the

Grasshopper Pie which is a mint ice cream with Oreos and a fudge swirl. Many people get the Maple Cream and pair that with the Brown Sugar Oatmeal for a great mix of flavors – and they do go together very nicely (I know because that's exactly what I got to eat after I spoke with Lisa).

Lisa says that "people love coming here because it's not on the main road, it's a nice quiet place to come and sit." The cows are right next to the stand if you'd like to see them as well. People return to Ilsley's because of the great flavors, but also the relaxing atmosphere. Lisa loves making people happy – you can't be mad when you're working with ice cream and making people happy. Her real passion is supporting the dairy industry, so the work directly impacts that, and she loves promoting local dairy.

Lisa enjoys creating new flavors, and, when I visited, she had recently made a lemon crumble which is a lemon ice cream with graham cracker, and it went over very well. So, she'll likely be making that again in the future. Ilsley's also makes their own waffle cones, and it was one of the best waffle cones I've ever had. You're sure to find something here you'll love. Visit soon to find out which flavor that is.

Attractions in the area:

Horace Lake Chase Park,
Clough State Park

Visit Ilsley's at
33 S Sugar Hill Road
Weare, NH 03281

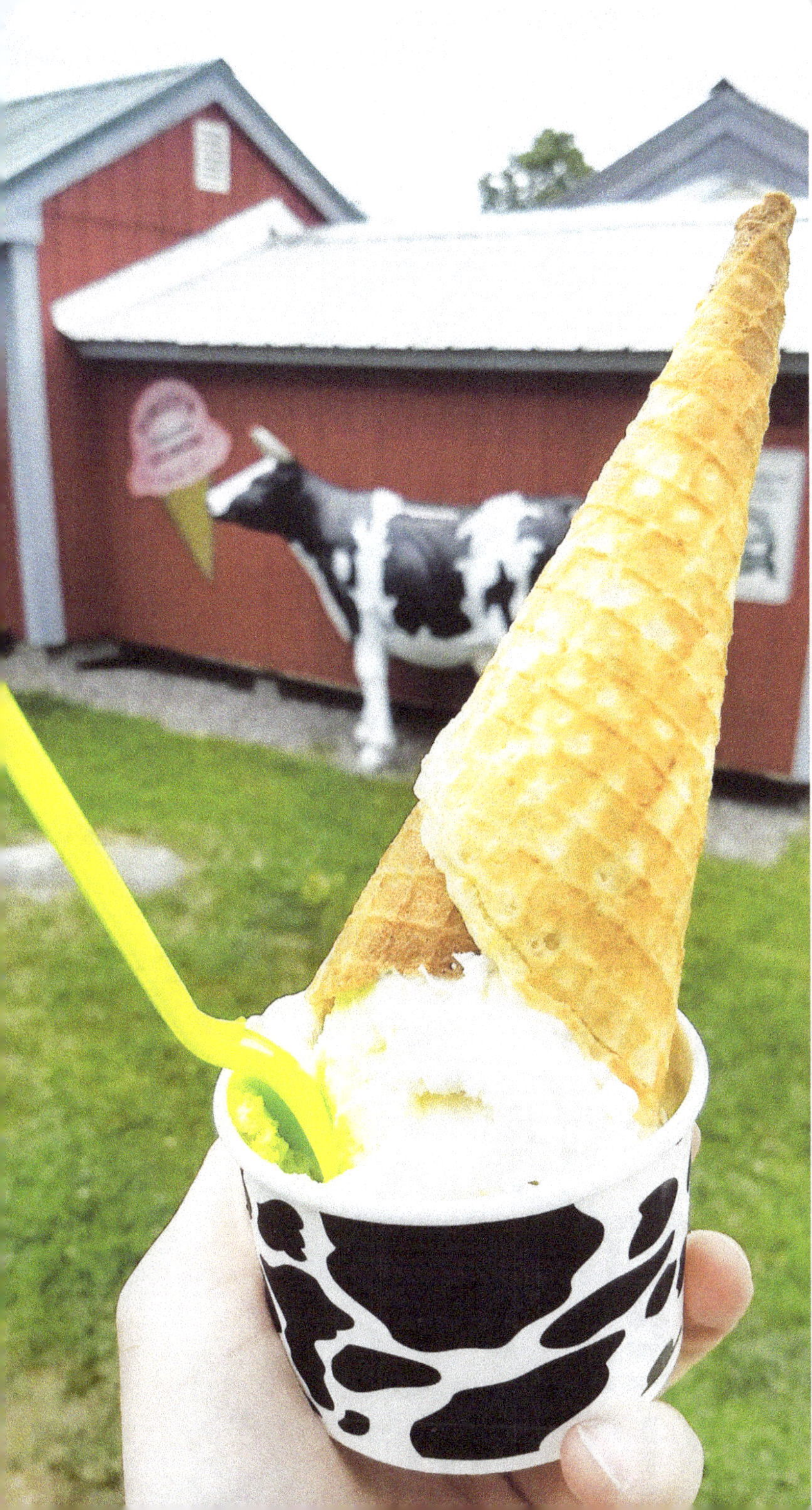

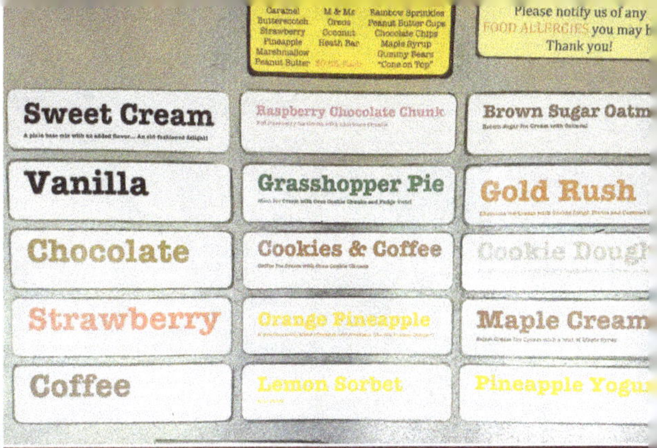
Caramel
Butterscotch
Strawberry
Pineapple
Marshmallow
Peanut Butter
M & Ms
Oreos
Coconut
Heath Bar
Rainbow Sprinkles
Peanut Butter Cups
Chocolate Chips
Maple Syrup
Gummy Bears
"Cone on Top"
Please notify us of any
FOOD ALLERGIES you may
Thank you!
Sweet Cream
Raspberry Chocolate Chunk
Brown Sugar
Vanilla
Grasshopper Pie
Gold Rush
Chocolate
Cookies & Coffee
Cookie
Strawberry
Orange Pineapple
Maple Cream
Coffee
Lemon Sorbet
Pineapple

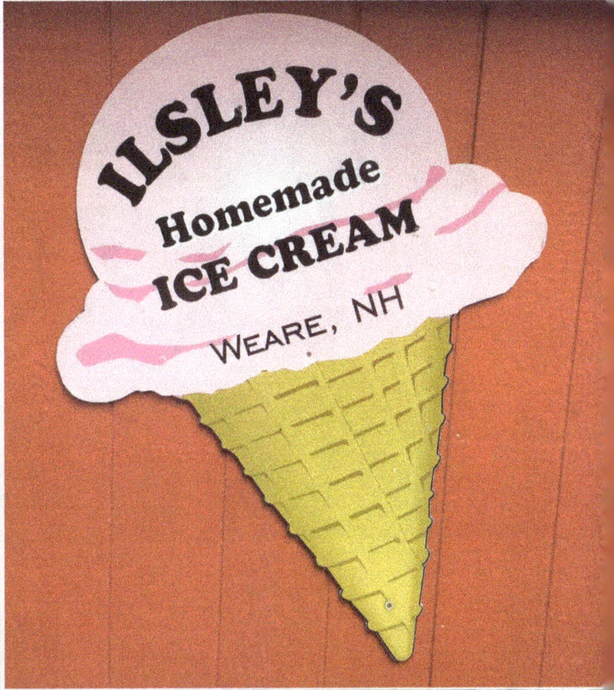
ILSLEY'S
Homemade
ICE CREAM
WEARE, NH

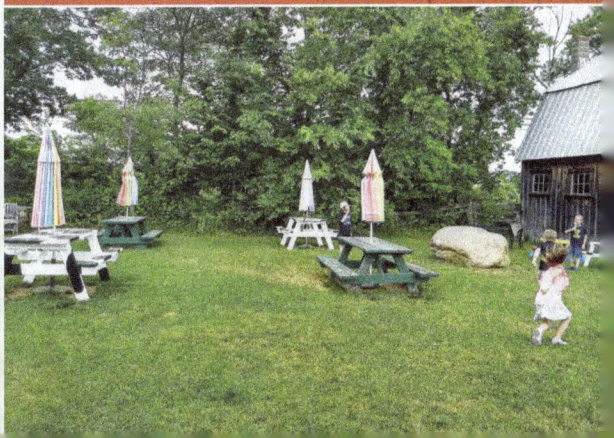

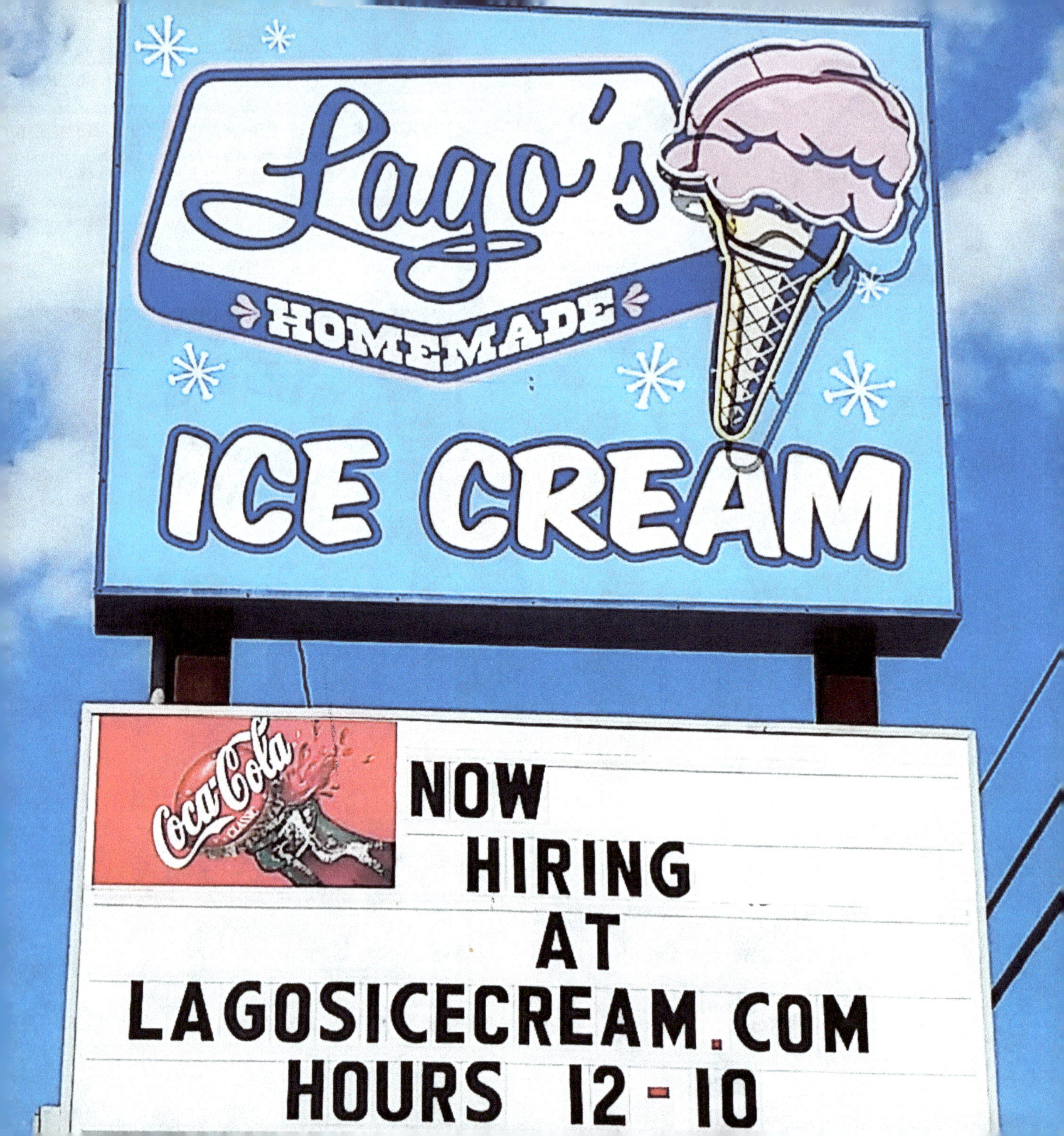
Lago's
HOMEMADE
ICE CREAM
Coca-Cola
NOW
HIRING
AT
LAGOSICECREAM.COM
HOURS 12-10

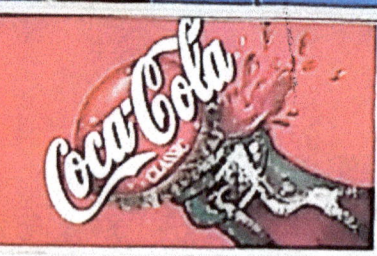

Lago's Ice Cream

RYE, NH

Mike and Carol Lago purchased Lago's in 1981. It was then incorporated. During the same year, Steve Grenier learned to make ice cream from his wife's grandfather. Andrea and Steve Grenier purchased the property in 2010. Steve's son has been making ice cream with him for the last 12 years or so.

Steve loves that he can create anything, and he often puts whatever he wants together at any time to come up with new flavors. He spoke about the Salty Sailor, a salted caramel ice cream with chocolate covered pretzels and the Beach Brownie which is a bourbon vanilla ice cream with chunks of homemade brownies, a red raspberry swirl, and toasted coconut.

A few of the more unique flavors are the Bovine So Fine which is a chocolate mint ice cream with Oreos and a fudge swirl and the Oatmeal Cream Pie, a brown sugar ice cream with chunks of Little Debbie oatmeal cream pies. Salty Sailor was started about four years ago and was named for the tall ships that come into Portsmouth every summer. Vanilla is most commonly ordered due to all of the frappes and sundaes served. The most requested flavor is the Black Raspberry Oreo, and the Mint Chocolate Chip is also a huge seller.

Steve thinks the dynamic of our seasons contribute to the large uptick in ice cream sales during the summer. People who want homemade ice cream tend to wait through winter until the shops open back up again and they are eager to get back out of the house and enjoy the day.

Steve talked about the quality of ingredients used at Lago's. He said it's about "making sure you get the value for the product you're putting out" so family and tourists can come out and enjoy it. "I think we make one of the best ice creams for the money you can get." Steve loves their funky selection of flavors and that's part of the reason people keep coming back to Lago's. The Kahlua Fudge Brownie uses real Kahlua and they always purchase quality and name brand items. He doesn't believe that one specific flavor draws customers in, but that the large selection and quality of the product does that.

I spent some time sampling a few flavors and I know what I'm lining up for my next trip. Scotty Lago's Bronze Run is very similar to a 7-layer bar, and that'll be my first order, shortly followed by my server Jillian's favorite, the Cookie Monster, which in Lago's case includes Chips Ahoy, Oreos, and Animal Crackers. On this trip, I went with the German Chocolate Cake as well as the previously mentioned Salty Sailor. One other interesting flavor I sampled was the Apple Cider Donut. It's seasonal and limited, so get it if you have the chance. The donuts are made by Donut Love, just down the street from Lago's.

In thirty-seven years of making ice cream, Steve never gets tired of it. "Creating something that puts a smile on someone's face," he says, "how can't you be happy about that?" A lot of work and hours go into this business and he enjoys making ice cream, but his time is spent on the management side, where his son has taken over the reins of making the ice cream. They love creating flavors that no one else has and when he puts it on Facebook, he loves the excitement that it stirs. Doing things like that and staying involved with the customers keeps him going and brings lots of enjoyment to the entire staff.

There are plenty of reasons to enjoy Lago's including the indoor and outdoor seating, plentiful parking and open field, as well as the over sixty-five flavors on hand at any one time, sets them apart from others. Lago's doesn't distribute, so plan your next trip to the seacoast around your stop here and find out why everyone keeps coming back!

Attractions in the area:

Odiorne Point State Park, Seacoast Science Center, whale watching.

Visit Lago's Ice Cream online at
www.lagosicecream.com
or they are located at
71 Lafayette Road
Rye, NH 03870

Coneheads

NORTH WOODSTOCK, NH

Tucked away in North Woodstock is an ice cream parlor worthy of a long drive. Myles Moran opened up Coneheads twenty-two years ago as a scoop shop. After about fifteen years, Myles began taking steps toward making their own homemade ice cream. Myles will be the first to tell you that making the switch to homemade ice cream has been the biggest asset to the business. During that time they put on a couple of additions to keep up with the increasing demand for their product.

There is quite some distance between Coneheads and the next closest ice cream parlor that makes their own ice cream, but Coneheads also makes their own flavors. They make their own chocolate, raspberry, and blueberry base flavors. Salted Caramel Pecan is a bit different, many places have a Salted Caramel flavor, but I struggle to think of another that uses pecans mixed in. Some other flavors of note are the Espresso Oreo and the Raspberry Truffle both of which you may find variations of at other locations, but these recipes are particular to Coneheads, designed and tested to the satisfaction of many.

The children love Cookie Monster, which tends to change from place to place. At Coneheads, the blue colored vanilla base has Oreos and chocolate chip cookies mixed in. Some of the more unique flavors include Banana Oreo, Barefoot Brownie - a vanilla base with a chocolate fudge swirl and chunks of fudge brownies mixed in, Ginger Snap ice cream - a ginger base ice cream with gingersnap cookies in it, and Pretzelogic – a vanilla ice cream with a caramel swirl and chocolate covered yogurt pretzels. I wasn't walking away without scoops of the Blueberry Cheesecake and the Chocolate Lovers.

All in all, coneheads produces approximately forty flavors of ice cream, but that's not all they make. Coneheads makes their own hard serve low-fat yogurts, Italian water ice, and a dairy-free product made with fresh fruit, water, sugar, and vegetable stabilizers. In addition to that, they make their own waffle cones and brownies for their brownie sundaes.

The Vanilla and Orange Pineapple flavors are very popular. As are the Root beer floats – yes they make those here too! All Jammed Up, run by Nicole Tewksbury, is a local fruit provider that Coneheads uses when berries are in season. "When you start with quality ingredients, you end up with a quality product," says Myles. Take the Maple Walnut ice cream for example. The maple syrup comes from Benton's Sugar Shack out of Thornton (and former Carlisle Award winner for best maple syrup producer in the state). Each five gallon batch of the Maple Walnut has a full quart of maple syrup in it to go along with the vanilla base and the walnuts, and nothing else to leave a brilliant maple taste.

Myles thinks we eat the most ice cream because we have the longest, coldest winters. On its face, it doesn't seem to make sense but he thinks that the ice cream sales from the stores pick up a lot when people are cooped up, and when it finally gets warmer and everyone heads out to the parlors in droves.

They use a flavoring system for their soft serve ice cream made with natural ingredients, if you really want that or if you have a picky eater in the family, but you're here for the good stuff.

Myles loves making the ice cream, and he has plenty of people who want to buy it, but Coneheads doesn't distribute, so if you want their ice cream, you need to make the trip. It's beautiful up in this area of New Hampshire though, and every bite of ice cream is worth it.

ATTRACTIONS IN THE AREA:

Lost River Gorge, Clark's Trading Post (museums, fire trucks, autos, all ages), water parks, zip lines.

Visit Coneheads online at
www.coneheadsnh.com
or they are located at
104 Main Street
North Woodstock, NH 03262

Bobby Sue's

FREEDOM, NH

Bobby Sue's started originally in 1987 in Ossipee. Later it changed ownership and was moved to Freedom. Autumn and Thatcher Graves purchased the parlor in 2012. Autumn had been working at the parlor since she was fourteen years old and the owners offered it to her when they were getting ready to retire. Going out for "ice cream is an experience, especially for homemade ice cream," says Thatcher. He believes they make a great product but thinks people come out for ice cream just for the experience.

One of the things Thatcher enjoys is creating new flavors. He has been working with a lot of peanut butter flavors since many of his employees and customers enjoy them. He told me about a peanut butter Oreo with a fudge swirl that he had made the prior night; it was given the name Peanut Butter Galaxy. A few people have requested a peanut butter & mint combination ice cream, but he hasn't tested those waters yet. No doubt if Thatcher ever gives that a try, it'll be an acquired taste.

Vanilla is the most popular flavor, particularly because of those going for sundaes, but Black Raspberry and Cookie Dough tend to be the bigger sellers here, and of course all the peanut butter flavors. Thatcher believes that the tourism is what pushes New Hampshire so far up the list when it comes to eating ice cream, but thinks a few of us try to fit in as much as possible before winter hits. I can attest to that; I've on more than one occasion hit the parlors up for discounted season end ice cream with the intent to eat it over the next 4-6 weeks. Reality sets in quickly when it only lasts a few days...

A lot of people come back for the Coffee Heath Bar and the Pistachio ice creams as well. I recommend the Pistachio; it's delicious. My personal favorites were the Lemon Chocolate Chip and Cookie Oreo.

Bobby Sue's tends to open in April and closes around Columbus Day, but stay updated as it's generally weather dependent. Given that there are only a few scoop shops in the area, and even fewer that make their own ice cream, Bobby Sue's tends to pull in people from a much wider range than many other shops in the state. Bobby Sue's does distribute to a few other scoop shops in the area including Trails End and Bly Farm. In addition to that, you can find pints and quarts at Sherman Farm in East Conway.

Some of the other things that Bobby Sue's makes are their own waffle cones and occasionally they make ice cream sandwiches. They have a menu item called the Mount Washington which is a bigger version of a banana split. One of my favorite tastings at Bobby Sue's was their Alamint flavor, which is one of the more unique offerings. It's a Mint Ice Cream with Oreos, chocolate chips, and a marshmallow swirl. The Cookie Jar flavor is a great selection as well if you like your add-ins; it has Oreos and M&M's in it.

Bobby Sue's also makes all of their own frozen yogurt, sorbet, and sugar-free ice creams. For dairy-free customers, they have coconut milk ice creams as well. Another amenity they offer is indoor seating which means no rainy day can ever keep you away.

Many of the customers come from nearby campgrounds, so if you're looking to pack a tent for a weekend getaway, consider checking out Bobby Sue's.

Distribution:

Available at scoop shops such as Trails End and Bly Farm. Also look for pints and quarts at Sherman Farm in East Conway.

Attractions in the area: '

Ossipee Lake, hiking in the valley, campgrounds

Visit Bobby Sue's at
70 Eaton Road
Freedom, NH 03836

BOBBY SUE'S ICE CREAM at COZY CORNER

The Mill Ice Cream Café and Fudge Factory
BRISTOL, NH

David Munro and Linda Carmichael purchased a historic building in 2005 and they renovated it for about a year before opening for business in August of 2006. After speaking to people in town and looking at options for a business they thought an ice cream parlor would be a good addition to the town. They started making homemade ice cream and quickly brought in fudge from the beginning and focused on those two items. They've since expanded to bring in espresso coffee, baked goods, and frappes.

The Mill Ice Cream Café and Fudge Factory makes their own cream base mix and they actually change that recipe depending on what flavor of ice cream is being made. They have five different recipes for their cream base mixes; I really haven't heard of anything else like that in my journey for this book. Their ice cream is made with only five ingredients. Ice cream is a perishable product, and they don't use anything that lengthens shelf life as they don't distribute and they don't keep it long. Vanilla is the most popular and it has a strong flavor; they don't use imitation vanilla there.

People keep coming back to the The Mill Ice Cream Café and Fudge Factory because they make their ice cream from scratch and in small batches. They have a special machine that mixes ingredients into their ice cream after it's been frozen. I had a scoop of Cookies and Cream that tasted super refreshing, which seems a bit odd I suppose in that a chocolate cookie isn't typically described in such a fashion, but the ice cream itself was exactly that.

The fudge here is just as great as the ice cream. It's also made from scratch and they have some amazing flavors. I'm not typically a fudge kind of guy. It tends to be just too sweet for me. I'm not sure if certain fudge makers add more sugar than the Factory or if it's the fact that many fudge makers use corn syrup in their products, which leaves an aftertaste. What I do know is that the Mill Ice Cream Café and Fudge Factory does not use corn syrup in their products and I have no problem eating this fudge. I had much more than I should have on a day I brought some to my workplace, and I wouldn't normally be able to eat fudge like that from other places. I had the Salted Caramel, the Raspberry, and the Johnnie Walker Red Label Scotch Whisky.

If you're looking for a parlor that sets themselves apart from the rest, The Mill Ice Cream Café and Fudge Factory needs to be on your list. One thing they do here that you won't find anywhere else, at least in New Hampshire, is that they add their fudge to three of their ice cream flavors – the Vanilla, Chocolate, and Coffee. Each flavor has up to five random flavors of fudge. It's an out of this world combination that I hadn't heard about before and it was a great experience.

People have told them that their Coconut, Coffee, and Chocolate Fudge ice creams are why they keep coming back, and they all sell very well. David told me that "people appreciate it when someone doesn't cut corners" and he enjoys "serving top quality product like that, something that you can't just get anywhere."

They make their own whipped cream and the signature product here is definitely the fudge - it's nationally acclaimed. Also, they have the Back Room at the Mill, which is a seating area with tables, that is set up for Friday night open microphone acoustic bands and there are often bands or events going on there during the summer. Bristol is a small town, and it has that small town feel; however, it has a truly bright light within its borders that should bring it more attention than it probably gets, and that's the the Mill Ice Cream Café and Fudge Factory.

Attractions in the area:

Wellington State Park, Profile Falls

Visit the Mill Ice Cream Café and
Fudge Factory online at
www.themillfudgefactory.com
or they located at
2 Central Street
Bristol, NH

Lone Oak

ROCHESTER, NH

Lone Oak was originally founded in 1962 by Ernest and Vasillia Bellemeur. They started with a small shop and there have been additions over the years. It was called Lone Oak because when the lot was cleared to make room, there was a single lone oak. In 1976 it was purchased by the current owners Michael and Carol Lago. It used to be the main route of travel before Route 16 was put in so it used to be bumper to bumper and many people would stop in. Now those people figure out how to get here from the highway so they can bring their children for some amazing ice cream.

Lone Oak is known for their homemade ice cream and large portions and I speak from experience when I've found this place absolutely packed with those seeking some of the best ice cream in the region.

For unique flavors, they've made everything from Chocolate Chocolate Bacon - a dark chocolate ice cream with chocolate covered bacon to Kettlecorn ice cream. Their Wookie Dough is a brownie batter-based ice cream with brownie dough pieces and chocolate chip cookie dough chunks. It's a flavor that is currently a special as I write this and may end up being a mainstay on the menu. This has happened so often with some of their flavors that they're finding it hard to fit in everyone's favorites. Cow Pie is an example of a new flavor that ended up staying for good. It's made with a brownie batter ice cream with homemade brownies chunks, chocolate chips, and a chocolate swirl. Manager Ken Viel notes there is a fine balance "between retaining some tradition and keeping up with the times."

Ken scours the web looking for new ideas and is always buying new ingredients to try new things. Vanilla is the most used flavor here by volume; the Chocolate, Kahlua Fudge Brownie, and the Mocha Chip sell very well as well. Rum Raisin, Frozen Pudding, and the Ginger also do surprisingly well.

This is the closest homemade ice cream to my house, so I eat here regularly. Cow Pie is one of my favorite flavors, but the Toasted Coconut and Butter Crunch are brilliant. Dairy is a big industry in New Hampshire and Ken believes that's why we love the ice cream here so much, but homemade ice cream is something people go out of their way for.

Lone Oak has a wide regional area of people who know about it. That's due in part to their great ice cream, but also because they have such a long history in the area. Lone Oak makes their own pies and brownies for their ice cream and sundaes. They also make their waffle cones. They get their maple syrup locally and also try to source fruit when it's in season. Lone Oak offers sugar-free ice cream, frozen yogurt, sorbet, and soft serve. They also offer a non-dairy almond milk soft serve.

Ken's favorite thing about making the ice cream is the creativity aspect of making something that no one has had before and he loves hearing from the customers about how amazing it is they are still around and how they used to come as a child or how they used to work at Lone Oak many years ago. He attributes that to a great staff even though it's a tough business for employment and turnover, given that much of the staff are in school. Ken loves that "people still want to come home" to Lone Oak. Come home to Lone Oak this summer and get some amazing ice cream at a great price.

Attractions in the area:

Jet Pack Comics, Rochester Opera House, Collectiques, Revolution Brewing

Visit Lone Oak online at
www.loneoakicecream.com
or they are located at
175 Milton Road
Rochester, NH 03868

Granite State Candy Shoppe
CONCORD, NH

The aroma is the first thing that hits you when walking into the Granite State Candy Shoppe. I had been by the chocolatier and ice cream parlor once or twice in the past but I was generally rushing to or from some other place. In doing so, I never noticed just how big it was. Jeff Bart is the owner. He grew up around the shop, went to college, and then came back to eventually help run the business again. Jeff's grandfather opened the shop in 1927. It served mainly hard candies and other things such as almond butter crunch. They had ice cream originally, but during World War II they stopped making it. About fifteen years ago, they started making ice cream again and the residents of Concord have benefited ever since.

Tal Smith is the general manager of Granite State Candy Shoppe and has been working there for over eight years. Granite State Candy Shoppe gets their base cream mix from Bohannan Farm and Contoocook Creamery which provides a 16% butterfat mix.

They make some of their own flavors from scratch at the shop, and try to source locally when possible. They get fresh strawberries when they can and for the Peppermint ice cream, they use candy cane that they make themselves, and of course, it has a great pink color. They also try to put in natural ingredients anywhere they can. A local shop, The Crust and Crumb, makes the sandwich portion of their ice cream sandwiches. Gould Hill Farm supplies peaches and apples.

Some of their more unique flavors include Flapjacks and Bacon. Edward Brand, the man who makes the ice cream, is looking to expand their cheesecake ice cream flavors. If the Blueberry Cheesecake flavor is available, take advantage of it. I loved the Mexican Chocolate which is a cinnamon chocolate flavor. Granite State Candy

Shoppe has a "make your own sundae" option, which means vanilla is the most popular flavor. I've only seen a toppings bar at one other location on my journey. The toppings bar has been around the last three years and has been a hit. They have a Maple Pecan in lieu of a Maple Walnut, which I'm in favor of, and they also have an Indian Pudding. The Salted Caramel and Coffee Oreo is a popular combination here, and if you try them together, you'll understand why. I'm a sucker for Orange Creamsicle, so I had a giant scoop of that.

Among the chocolates (of which I walked out with quite a few) is something unique if you want to leave with a treat for later and that's the Pub Brittle which consists of peanuts, pretzels, and beer.

"You can't really compare working in a candy shop to anything else," says Tal, and I'm sure there is much truth to that. I also spoke with Caleb Ruopp who remarked about the aroma and how it's one of the things he looks forward to when he comes into work.

Caleb says the hard part with ice cream is coming up with good names, but if the name is too fanciful, people don't know what it is and then they may not order it. Edward was telling me about a great experience he had at the Made in New Hampshire Expo where he had created the flavor, Flantastic Crunch. A customer tried it who grew up eating flan in his home country and was thrilled with the result. While that flavor isn't currently on the menu, the dedication to getting something like that right pays off, and you taste that quality and effort in all of the flavors at the Granite State Candy Shoppe.

Distribution:

Huntoon Farm sells their ice cream. Deerfield Fair purchases many cases as well.

Attractions in the area:

Discovery Museum, Historical Society, Barley House

Visit the Granite State Candy Shoppe online at
www.granitestatecandyshoppe.com
or they are located at
13 Warren Street
Concord, NH 03301

Dudley's HOMEMADE ICE CREAM

SANDWICHES ICE CREAM AND MORE

Dudley's Ice Cream

LOUDON, NH

Carolyn Dudley grew up around ice cream. Dudley's Ice Cream is a family owned business and Carolyn's parents were serving soft serve ice cream back in 1971. Eventually, Dudley's opened at its current location in 1998 where they now make their own hard serve ice cream. At an early age, Carolyn knew that she was going to stay involved with something she loved so much, and she's often busy making the ice cream or traveling for events.

The quality of the ice cream is what brings people back to Dudley's. They have a Coconut Cream flavor here that is a must try and I paired that up with their Key Lime ice cream. I didn't stop there though. I sampled the Frozen Pudding, the Extreme Chocolate which is a serious, deep, dark chocolate - and quite tasty. The French Vanilla is a nice simple flavor if you don't want to go too crazy. Some of Dudley's other offerings include Rum Raisin which definitely hits the sweet spot, a Black Raspberry Truffle which is a black raspberry base with raspberry-filled truffles, and a Fudge Brownie.

After Vanilla, Mint Chip, Maple Walnut, and the Purple Cow are some of the more popular flavors at Dudley's. The maple syrup for the Maple Walnut is made locally. Dudley's doesn't shy away from creativity, however, as they've created quite a few unique flavors in the past including Buttered Caramel Popcorn, Blueberry Cobbler, and Stick in the Mud which is chocolate ice cream with cookie dough chunks and gummy worms.

Other things you can get at Dudley's include sugar-free ice cream, frozen yogurt, sundaes, frappes, floats, and slush puppies. It should be noted that you can come here for lunch as well because Dudley's makes many different kinds of subs and sandwiches. The chicken salad is homemade and is a local favorite. There is no need to be in a rush either as they have

plenty of outdoor seating. Dudley's also makes ice cream cakes and you can take home ice cream in pints and quarts as well. Keep track of their Facebook page as they sometimes host cruise nights for antique car enthusiasts.

Carolyn said that "we have a lot of ice cream stands and a lot of places that make their own ice cream" in New Hampshire and that's possibly why we eat so much of it. Perhaps there are more people out there like myself who want to try something from every ice cream stand they can find. Even in a complete downpour, Dudley's tends to bring people in, as I met a few people when I stopped by in what can only be described as buckets being dumped, but they would not be deterred by a simple thing such as rain.

Dudley's does switch out flavors from the menu every so often, but the favorites stay permanently. Carolyn finds many people tend to pick a flavor they like and stick with that for the most part. I've found throughout my trip that this does happen at quite a number of ice cream parlors. If you're looking for a good portion of ice cream at the right price, stop through Loudon and get a cone. You'll be happy that you did.

ATTRACTIONS IN THE AREA:

New Hampshire Motor Speedway, Canterbury Shaker Village in Canterbury

Visit Dudley's Ice Cream at
846 NH-106
Loudon, NH 03307

AT THE FARM

I worked on a dairy farm one day in my life, Steve Cole's farm just off of route 77 in southern New Jersey. It was a place that even read from the road "this is the home and property of hard work." My father had to go... somewhere. I can't remember where...it was some extra weekend work or something to try and make some ends meet. He left my younger brother Brett and at the farm to help out Steve for the day.

I loved this farm, not because I had spent some great amount of time there or because they had fifty different kinds of animals. I loved this farm because it had one of my favorite animals, an animal which I proudly shout out my windows is my friend. The cow is that animal. Steve's farm was a dairy farm, and he had a lot of cows. I still remember that day like it was yesterday. It was very hot, or at least very humid. The work was very hard. I learned one very important lesson that day. I was never getting a dairy farm.

Hatchland Farm

NORTH HAVERHILL, NH

If you're looking for a beautiful drive through the countryside on your way to some of the freshest ice cream you're likely to ever have, you can't do much better than Hatchland Farm in North Haverhill. One mile away from the ice cream shop is the farm itself where Dave and Kristen May have the tremendous undertaking of producing, processing, and bottling their own milk from over 300 cows. They took over the farm from Kristen's father who originally purchased it in 1971. He stayed true to his roots by not selling out when the government came knocking and instead looked for ways to expand.

Dave joined the farm in 1988 and has seen a lot of changes over the years. In 2011, after years of turning out extra cream which was sold off to other ice cream producers, they decided to make their move into ice cream. The first two seasons they purchased ice cream for their shop until they could learn to produce the ice cream themselves. Dave went to Penn State for their well-known ice cream short course and now enjoys churning out anywhere between 20-30 flavors made right on the farm. Since Hatchland Farm controls the entire process from the cows to the cone, you're unlikely to find a fresher ice cream anywhere else.

Hatchland Farm started with a 20-quart machine which they purchased from Walpole Creamery and ended up producing so much that they upgraded to a machine that does twice as much. I mentioned how I've never seen comments on an ice cream web page about the milk and Dave spoke to the pasteurization process they use. "The big companies heat their milk at a fairly high temperature for short time pasteurization," he said. "At Hatchland Farm, we heat it at a lower temperature for half an hour, which is obviously a more labor-intensive process - and often times how older and smaller farms pasteurize." It's clear that the process handled a different way does affect the taste.

Hatchland does make a few of their own flavors including any of their fresh fruit flavors. Blueberry Cinnamon Cake ice cream is one of these as well as a Chocolate Chili, which I had to try since I like spicy, and it's just the right amount of kick. Hatchland generally carries about twenty flavors or so, and the customers come back in droves for some of the more unique flavors in the fall such as Pumpkin and Apple Pie.

Maple Walnut and Black Raspberry are the more popular flavors here not named Vanilla or Chocolate. I had the Black Raspberry and it was spectacular. I also sampled the Banana, which was quite refreshing on what was a very hot day. If you're looking for something with a bit more punch, the Espresso Bean is quite good and you should know that the Peanut Butter Cup flavor is not a vanilla ice cream with peanut butter cups in it, but it's actually a peanut butter base ice cream with chocolate in it. For the cookies and cream, Dave didn't want to overdo it with the vanilla as that would take away from what the true flavor was supposed to be, so he crushed up cookies very finely to mix it in with the ice cream in addition to the larger chunks of cookies one is accustomed to.

Hatchland Farm will custom make ice cream cakes with two to three flavors and they also make their own waffle cones and whipped cream. While they don't make the cookie sandwiches, the ice cream in the cookie sandwiches does use their ice cream and they don't stay on the shelves long. If you live nearby consider stopping at the shop opposed to going to the window and check out the other local goods they offer from their farm as well as others in the area such as meats, cheeses, syrup, and of course, the Hatchland milk. The chocolate milk is wicked good!

Attractions in the area:

Polar Caves in Rumney, Windy Ridge Orchard & Christmas Tree Farm in Haverhill

Visit Hatchland Farm at
3095 Dartmouth College Highway
North Haverhill, NH 03774

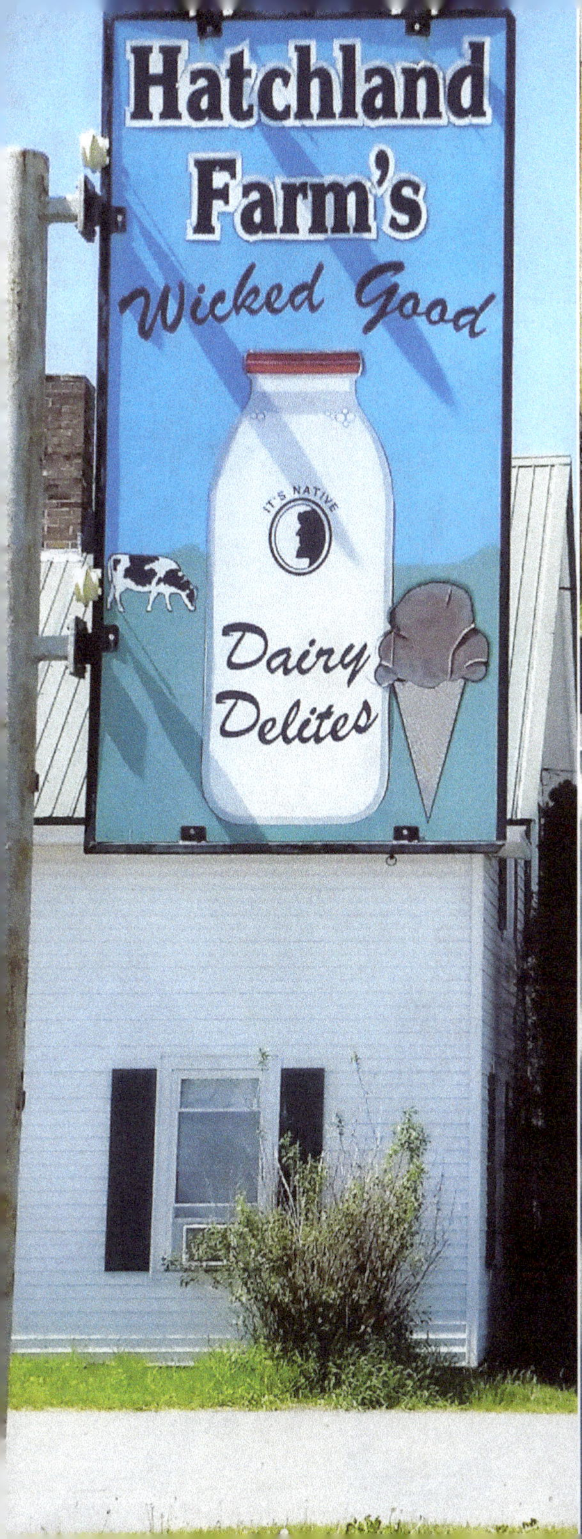
Hatchland
Farm's
Wicked Good
IT'S NATIVE
Dairy Delites

Hatchland Farm's
"Wicked Good"
Dairy Delites
& Milk Store
OPEN

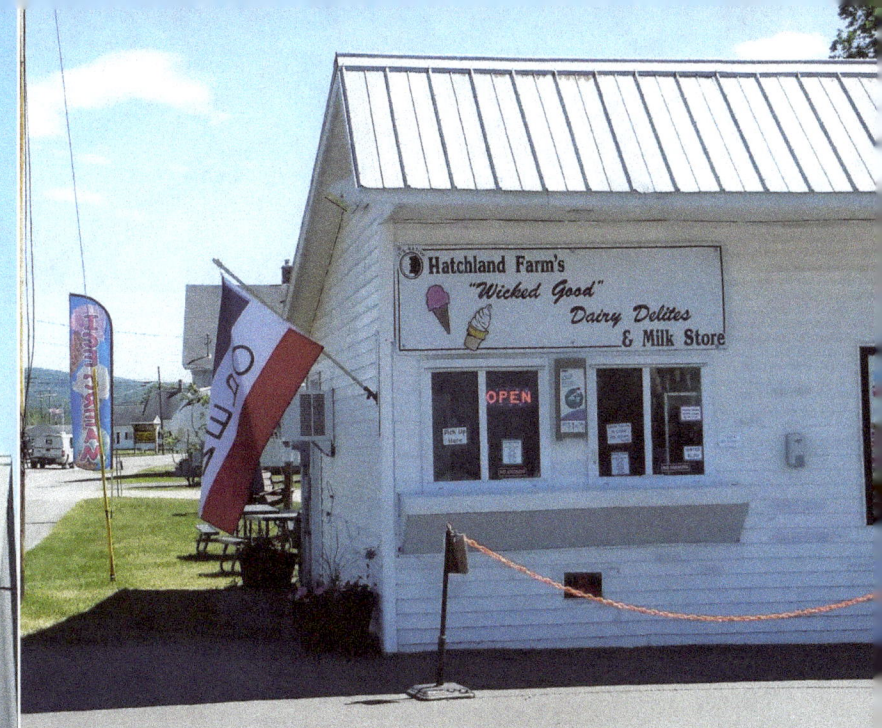

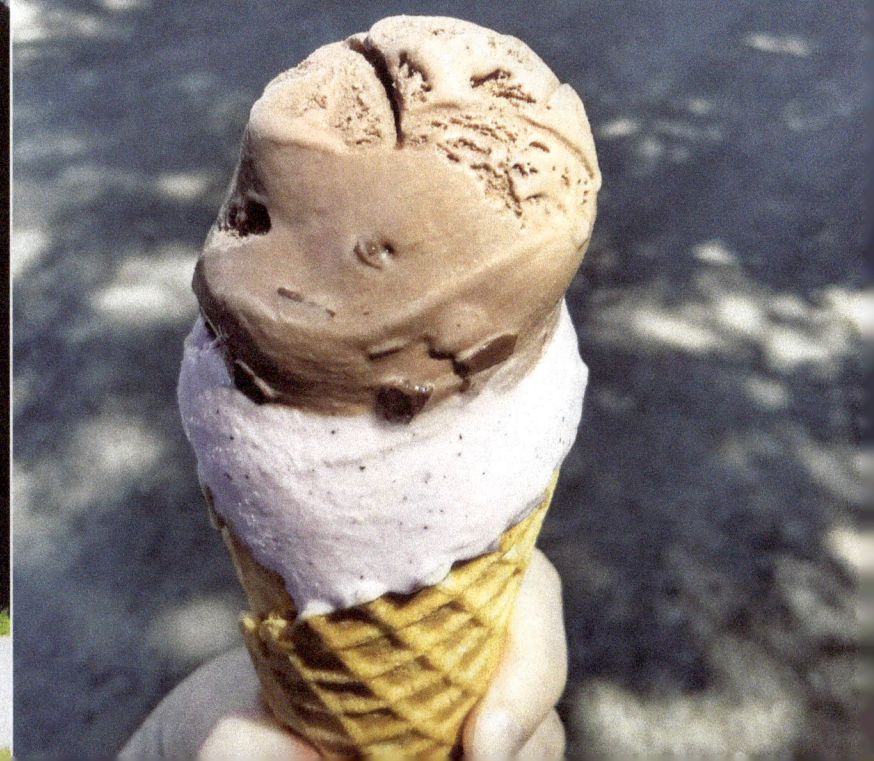

Sanctuary Dairy Farm

SUNAPEE, NH

Sanctuary Dairy Farm is a tenth-generation farm which opened its own ice cream shop in 2009 with a single dipping cabinet. The farm has approximately 100 head of cattle, 35-40 of which are milking cows. They slowly built themselves up to add more dipping cabinets, more flavors, and more toppings. Owner Beck Johnson originally sold ice cream from Walpole Creamery before making the move into homemade ice cream. He took a few courses from Malcolm Stogo, a well-known author, publisher, and parlor owner in the ice cream industry. Beck also took the ice cream short course from Penn State.

Sanctuary Dairy Farm does make their own flavors when they are in season. The more unique flavors are Maple Whiskey, the Caramel Cashew Chocolate Chip, and the Cappuccino Crunch, which is a light coffee-based flavor filled with toffee bar crunch pieces. They do rotate in special flavors periodically. While I was there, the two specials were Chocolate Cappuccino and Green Tea.

The Lemon Cookie is a refreshing flavor but the most popular flavors after Vanilla would be any of the maple flavors and the Cappuccino Crunch, as well as the Chocolate. The Cherry Chocolate Chip is also delightful. For dairy-free people, the coffee is a popular flavor and they do change the flavors up for the non-dairy folks so there is always something different. For daring larger groups, consider going with The Wrist Breaker, which is 20 scoops of ice cream with brownies and toppings.

Beck believes that the atmosphere of the ice cream shops in New Hampshire, being small businesses, opposed to chain stores, leads to some of the reason why people keep going back to eat so much ice cream. He thinks each shop has its own take or twist on things. Sanctuary Farms stands out

from the others because they embrace the farm culture and depend on the quality of their product. Beck says that "the farming culture is still prevalent," and Sanctuary Dairy Farm "offers a slice of what it's like to be on a farm."

Sanctuary Dairy Farm is an engaging place for children as they have goats right next to the stand and a partially fenced in play area for families that want to hang out for a while. "We try to have a nice fun area where customers can let their kids run free". Keep an eye out for Melvin the cat who is quite sociable at times. Among other things you'll see on your visit is a farm stand where they sell locally made products such as meats, cheese, and eggs among other items.

Sanctuary Dairy Farm does distribute ice cream to six farm stands throughout the state. They sell their ice cream wholesale to Beaver Pond Farm Stand and Eccardt Farm. Sanctuary Dairy Farm's milk is used in Cabot cheeses. There always seems to be a project going on at the farm to improve the farm or the ice cream parlor. While there is a lot to do and see at Sanctuary, the real attraction is the ice cream. There is a reason Sanctuary Dairy Farm has won New Hampshire Magazine's Best of Ice Cream in the region four years in a row. Come out to the farm and discover the reason this summer!

Attractions in the area:

The two biggest things are the mountain and the harbor. In spring time, the harbor is busy with boating/swimming/fishing/boat tours. The mountain has an adventure park/frisbee course and mountain biking. Restaurants are mostly in Newport.

Visit Sanctuary Dairy Farm online at
www.icecreamkidbeck.com
or they are located at
209 NH-103
Sunapee, NH 03782

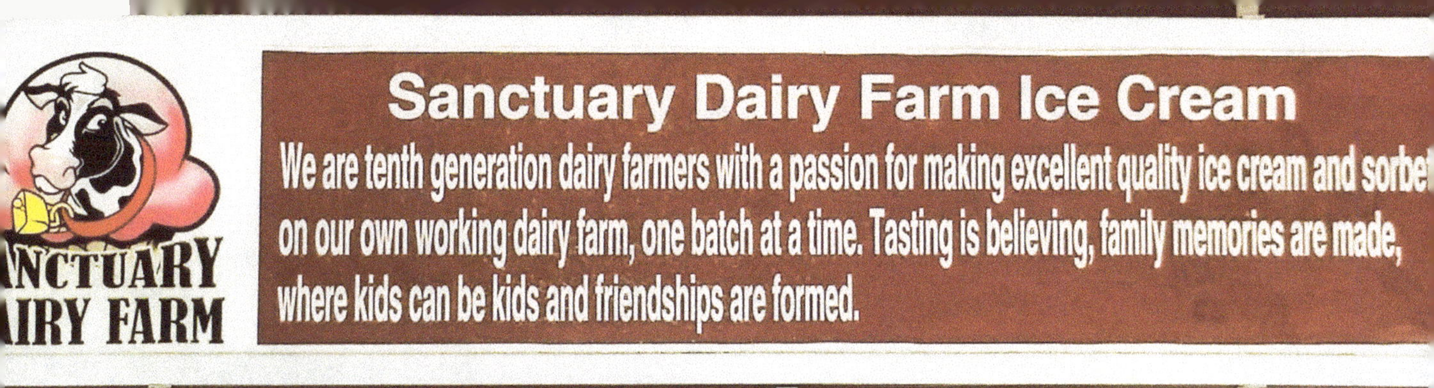

Sanctuary Dairy Farm Ice Cream

We are tenth generation dairy farmers with a passion for making excellent quality ice cream and sorbet on our own working dairy farm, one batch at a time. Tasting is believing, family memories are made, where kids can be kids and friendships are formed.

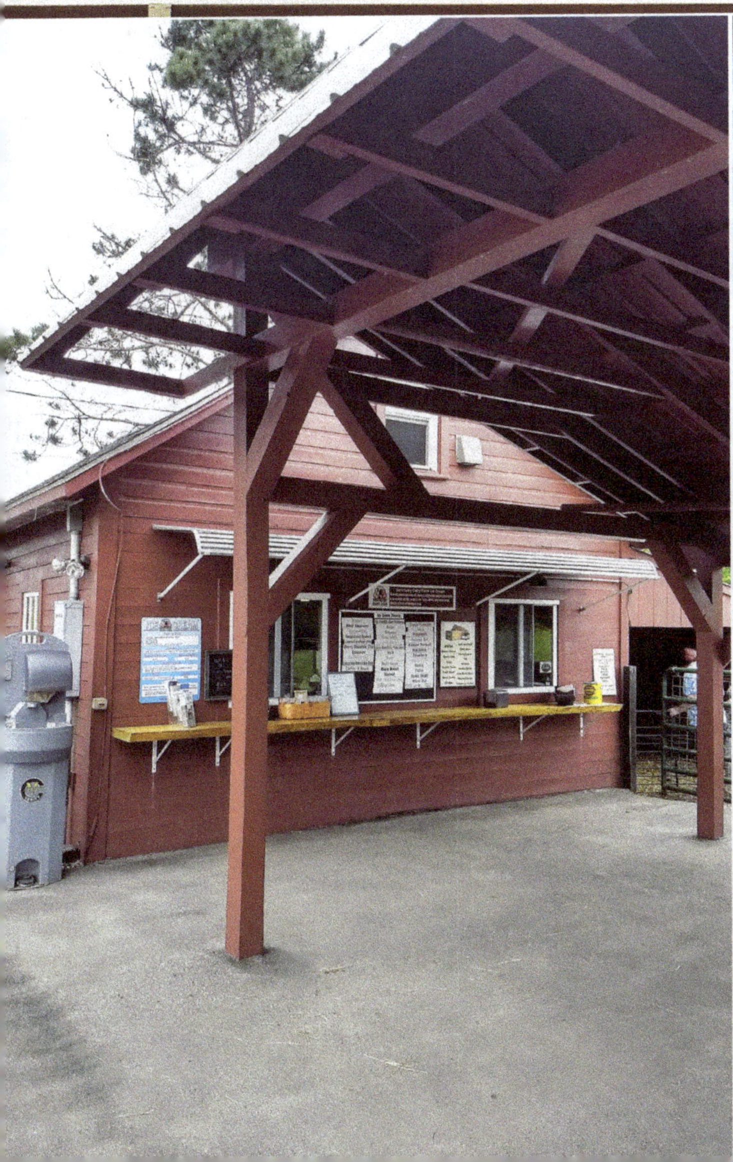

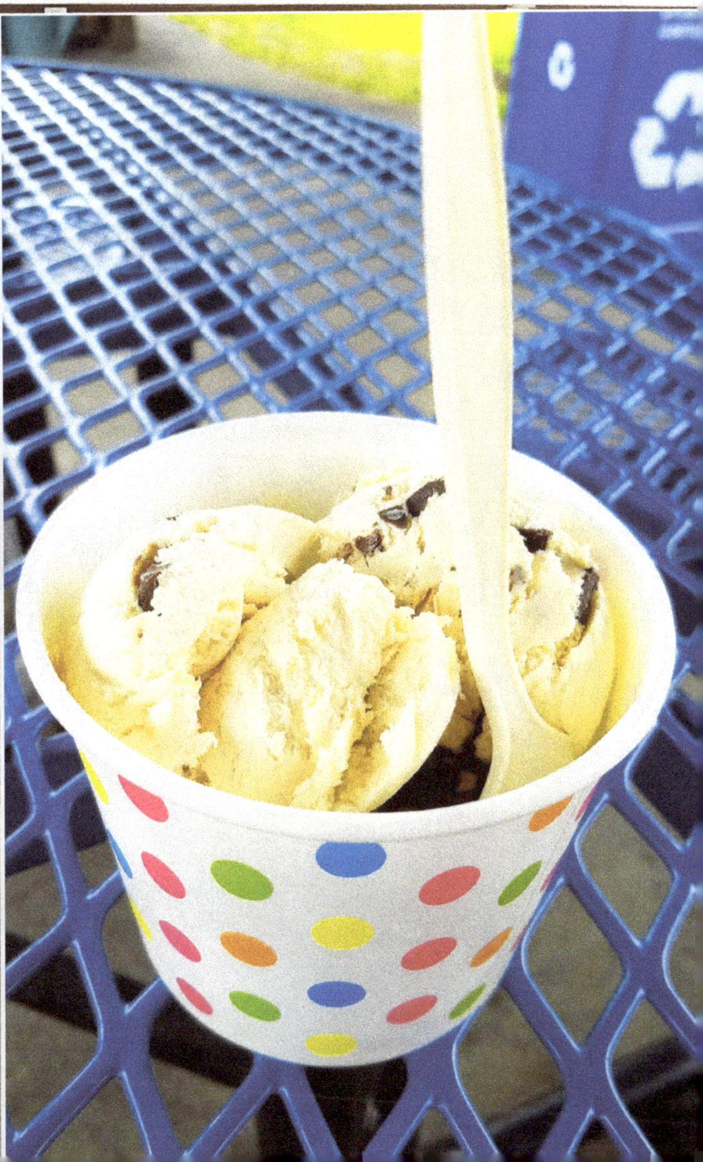

Richardson's Farm

BOSCAWEN, NH

Jim Richardson is a third generation owner of Richardson's Farm. His family lived on a farm from the 1700s until the 1920s down in Pelham. They were one of many smaller farms near urban areas. Up until 1907, the cash flow depended on surplus milk and the laws were changed that prevented raw milk from being sold. His grandfather moved off of that farm in 1907 and set up a bottling plant. In 1956, the farm started making ice cream and they've been making it ever since. Jim moved to the current location in 2001 where Richardson's continues making ice cream.

Richardson's is one of the few in the state who make their own base ice cream mix still. They believe people come back to Boscawen because they have the best ice cream in the state. They don't have a strong web presence and don't actively advertise, but instead rely on word of mouth. "We do have a following that is extremely loyal to the product we make," he says, and then jokes that they may not like him much, but they love the ice cream. For the record, Jim was one of the most enjoyable interviews I had and it's obvious that he takes what he does seriously even if he doesn't take himself seriously, which can be a bit of an endearing trait.

As Jim talks to me, we walk through the kitchen where they had just pulled some date squares and pies out of the oven. They make everything at Richardson's from scratch. The base usually consists of milk, cream, nonfat dairy solids, sugars and a stabilizer. The base can completely change depending on what type of combination used – and many times this can affect the taste of the ice cream more than the flavors. During my travels, this definitely proved to be true, but in the case of Richardson's Strawberry Rhubarb ice cream, I have nothing to compare it to as only one or two other places make the flavor, but this is obviously a seasonal most everywhere.

Katherine's Passion has an interesting story behind it. A frequent customer and friend came in three or four years ago and asked if Jim had ever heard of an ice cream that had cayenne pepper. He started messing around with a chocolate, cayenne, and cinnamon and named it after the one who suggested it. Apparently, she didn't come around for a couple weeks after that, slightly embarrassed at the insinuation she was "hot and spicy." Butter Rum ice cream, which is a butterscotch flavor with some rum and toffee pieces, is pretty unique and has a nice strong flavor.

Richardson's Farm has about ten flavors that are unique to them. They make their own raspberry topping, rhubarb topping and their own caramel topping – which I would recommend. It uses a lot of butterfat, but you don't find too many homemade caramel toppings, so if you enjoy caramel, it's worth the trip for this alone.

Other than their Vanilla (which has a great flavor), the most popular ice creams here are the Maple Walnut, Black Raspberry, and the Cookie Dough. For hotter days try the Banana or Rum Raisin. If Katherine's Passion isn't quite your type of spicy, try the Gingersnap. Jim isn't shy with the fact that he'd rather be out in the fields farming than making the ice cream; however, he feels as if he has a duty to continue running one of the few remaining parlors which makes not only the flavors but the base ice cream mix through the entire ice cream making process.

As if they aren't busy enough with the ice cream, Jim and Sue make their own waffle cones, pies, and a multi-berry sauce. The apple crisp and the pastry dough for all the pies are made from scratch on the premises. It was national chocolate ice cream day when I stopped at Richardson's Farm, so I felt pretty locked into a Chocolate Brownie Sundae after talking with Jim. If you're looking for something different though, try Wild Meggie's Mint Julip which is a bourbon with mint mix and thank me later.

ATTRACTIONS IN THE AREA:

Carter Hill Orchhard in Canterbury,
Hackleboro Orchards in Canterbury,
Brookford Farm in Canterbury

Visit Richardson's Farm online at
www.richardsonsfarmnh.com
or they are located at
170 Water Street
Boscawen, NH 03303

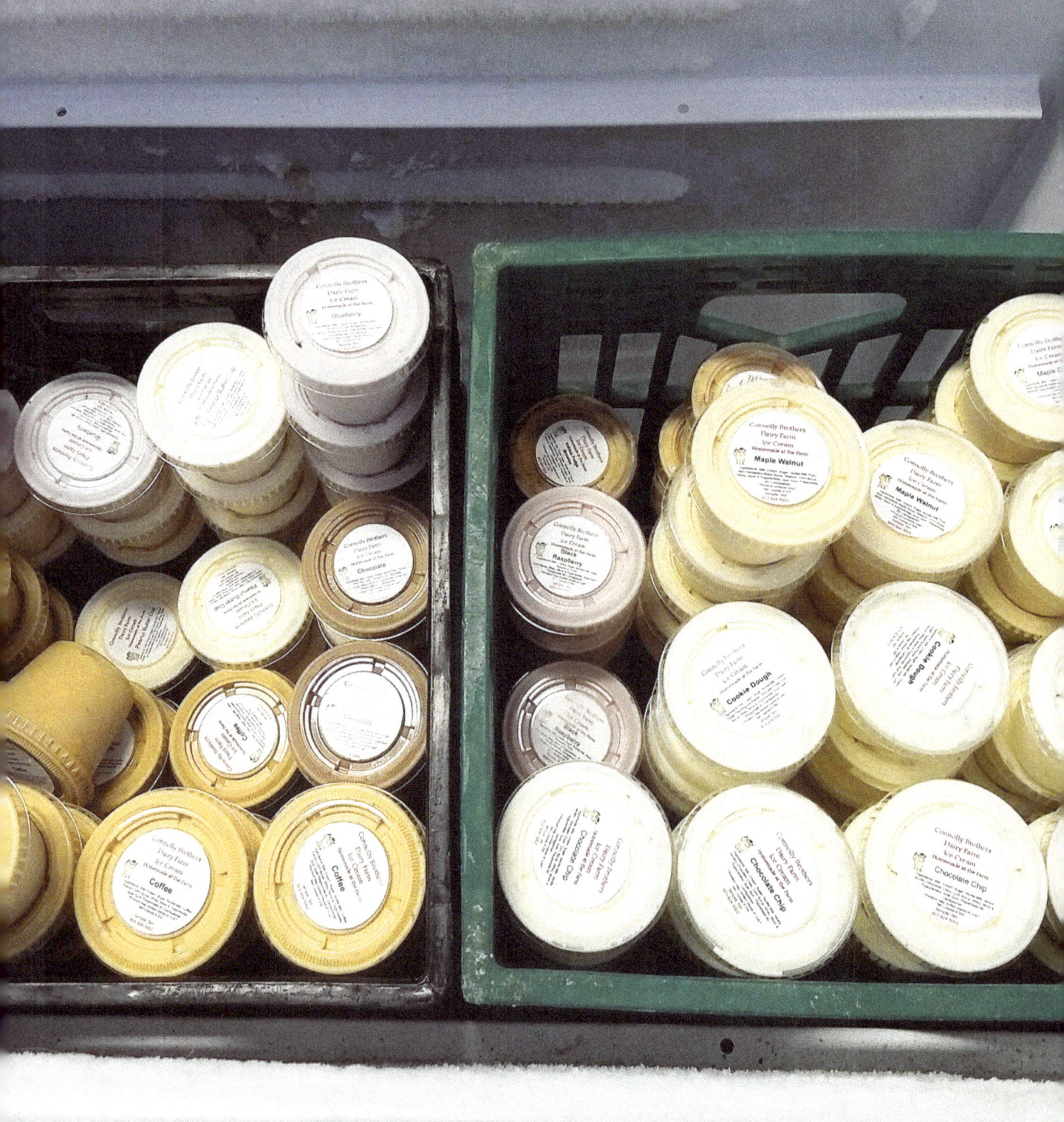

Connolly Brothers Dairy Farm

TEMPLE, NH

Chris, Mike, and Patrick Connolly purchased their dairy farm from their parents in 1996; at that point they were just a wholesale milk operation. Their parents had dabbled in ice cream back in the mid-1980s, but didn't maintain that as the brothers were all getting ready to head off to college. In 2000, knowing they would need to expand the services they offered, they decided to start moving into retail products. They started with raw milk and then in 2002 they saw an ad in the newspaper for an ice cream parlor which was selling all of their ice cream making equipment.

Even though making ice cream was only on the periphery of what they were looking to do, it seemed like the perfect opportunity to expand the products they were offering. They ended up diving in and purchasing two ice cream machines and other equipment they needed. In 2003, they started making their ice cream and have been doing so ever since. They don't scoop ice cream at the farm, but they sell packaged ice cream. They have single servings, half pints, pints, quarts, gallons and they do 2.5-gallon containers for some restaurants. They will; however, be opening a scoop shop soon, likely by the time this book is published, as they're currently working on finishing up a building for that and their farm stand as well.

Connolly Brothers Dairy Farm "produces roughly 200 gallons of ice cream a week during the summer time" according to Chris. The production has soared the last couple of seasons as Charlie's Old Tyme Ice Cream and another location in Vermont purchase a lot of ice cream from them. Many restaurants purchase seasonal ice creams that they make at the farm. The strawberries they use are from Barrett Hill Farm and they use their own maple syrup for all of their maple flavored ice cream. The blueberries they use are picked from the homestead as well.

For unique flavors try their Whoppers ice cream which has the well-known malted milk ball treats mixed in. Sweet Piggy is their maple cream ice cream with caramelized bacon in it and this is a big hit. Coffee Heath Bar is one of the most popular sellers along with any of their maple flavors; likely because the customers know that the syrup is coming right from the farm. One of the things the farm is known for is their ice cream sandwiches. They make their own cookies to put with their ice cream and they do not stay on the shelves for very long. I would have tried one, but they were all sold out when I got there.

I grabbed up a whole bunch of the single serving cups for sampling. The Kahlua Fudge Brownie is a great selection for the chocolate lover and the Coffee Heath Bar was everything it should be. I had the Maple Walnut which really isn't a flavor I try very often even though I love maple syrup and I rather enjoyed that one. The Mint Chocolate Chip is excellent, but the Blueberry was the real surprise for me, and I found myself seeking to finish that one as soon as possible.

Chris loves the customers' excitement when they come in for the ice cream and Connolly Brothers Dairy Farm does make ice cream throughout the year until about New Years. While they slow down production in the winter and early spring, they do continue to make it since they have customers who come on a regular basis for their other farm products. They sell their own milk, cheeses, and meats among other things. The cows are around if you want to say hi and the farm does ship milk, so only some of their milk is used in the ice cream. Their goal is to eventually use only their own milk for their ice cream. This is the kind of farm everyone wants in their town, and you'll understand why when you arrive!

ATTRACTIONS IN THE AREA:

Frye's Measure Mill, downtown Peterborough, North State Park

Visit Connolly Brothers Dairy Farm at
140 Webster Highway
Temple, NH 03084

Sandwich Creamery

NORTH SANDWICH, NH

Tom Merriman opened Sandwich Creamery in 1995 where they primarily made cheese to start and soon followed that up with ice cream on the side. The ice cream sales have picked up tremendously. The property was built as a farm specifically with the idea of making it into a creamery. Tom already had some cows and other animals around and wanted to work closer to home so that's what gave him the idea to get this started. One thing that makes the creamery stand out, other than being a farm in North Sandwich (what many would say is "in the middle of nowhere"), is the honor system for their products. Upon entering the storefront you'll notice that there is no one at a register, just a basket for your payment. You get whatever products you want and pay for it. You can't get quicker service than that - and if the service is slow you only have yourself to blame!

The Sandwich Creamery has around thirty flavors of ice cream and they do make a few sorbets as well. They are going to start making some coconut milk ice cream for those who can't have dairy as the demand for that product seems to be picking up. Tom loves seeing the customers who make the trip out to the creamery as they're always in a good mood – as everyone is who comes out for ice cream. With it being on a farm and in a rural setting, it makes for a unique family trip. Ice cream is "an inexpensive outing" for the entire family to do and something after a workday or on the weekend according to Tom, which may explain why so many people in New Hampshire keep eating it – even during the cold months.

I spoke with Charly Moriarty, Tom's stepdaughter, who makes most of the ice cream at Sandwich Creamery and has been for around ten years. During the summertime, they'll bring in someone to help a bit and keep up with production.

Charly says she loves "when people come to visit and tell [her] how much they love the ice cream," especially since she plays the central role in creating it.

Chocorua Orange which is a chocolate base with orange extract, Tipsy Turtle which has caramel cups and pecans, a seasonal Eggnog ice cream and the Mexican Jumping Bean (a cinnamon chocolate with a bit of kick) are some of the more unique flavors. I haven't seen too many Lemon ice cream flavors, but Sandwich Creamery does offer a Lemon Squeeze. Cow Tracks (known as Moose tracks to most of us New Hampshirites) is a vanilla ice cream with chocolate fudge chunks and peanut butter cups and is their most popular flavor – as is their Vanilla ice cream.

Sandwich Creamery does sell wholesale to scoop shops. The Creamery has a Squam Sundae, named after the Squam Lake, which is a pre-made sundae with brownie, vanilla ice cream, hot fudge, walnuts and a cherry. It's only available on the weekends usually from a Friday to a Sunday. Charly said one thing that makes their place different is that some customers find the place because they got lost. If you decided to make this journey, you'll understand why she says this.

Sandwich Creamery is one of the few places I actually stopped at more than once this summer. Part of that is because of how amazing their ice cream is. Another part of that could be that I forgot to grab more than one flavor for sampling the first time I was there. It's a completely worthwhile trip, just for the beautiful drive – but you'll be more interested in the Chocolate, Bearcamp Blueberry and the Sea Salt Caramel, which are all simple yet robust flavors. If you're like me, you'll find yourself back at Sandwich Creamery a second time as well!

Attractions in the area:

Many hiking trails, this is a good spot to stop after some hiking, lots of good boating and swimming in the area, the Potholes (rocky river place to swim), Bee Falls, restaurant in town called the Corner House.

Visit Sandwich Creamery online at
https://sandwich-creamery.business.site
or they are located at
130 Hannah Road
North Sandwich, NH 03259

RESTAURANTS
"I'm hungrier than that..."

I can't count how many times I've eaten a large lunch or dinner and then said to myself, "Sure, I can fit in some ice cream." We've all probably done that once or twice or 200 times. Your stomach says, "please no," and your eyes say, "ice cream!" There is something about that silver spoon and silver bowl, neither of which are silver, which recalls memories of a greasy burger and a good time with friends or family.

I love food. Many people have asked me about what the best ice cream places are, or if I plan on writing any other books about food. Probably not. This was hard work, and even though I can write, it doesn't really mean that's what I want to do. I'm looking forward to working on a YouTube channel where I travel around the state and try different food (including ice cream of course). I'll continue this adventure in video form for everyone to enjoy, and I'm already looking forward to the eating part. Here are some ice cream destinations that include full lunch and/or dinner menus for those who are looking for more than just ice cream.

- Almond Joy Oreo
- Cookie Dough Dirty Water
- Maple Walnut Boston Blackout
- Graham Central Station
- Chocolate Cookie Monster
- Peanut Butter 180 Pistachio
- French Vanilla Moose Tracks
- Strawberry Fools Gold
- Columbian Coffee Cookie Jar
- Mint Chip Butter Pecan
- Chocolate Vanilla
- Walnut Fudge Black Raspberry
- Chocolate Chip Mocha Chip
- Cotton Candy Smores
- Cherry Vanilla Dino Crunch
- Dough Dough Brrr! (lite)
- Chocolate Crumb Cheesecake
- Mocha Chip Orange Sherbet
- Double Chocolate Chip
- Black Raspberry Chip Yogurt
- Mocha Toffee Chunk Yogurt

Blake's Restaurant & Ice Cream
MANCHESTER, NH

In 1900, Blake's was opened in Manchester by Edward Charles Blake. It was a dairy processor, which bought milk from local farmers and then bottled it for delivery to nearby homes. In 1963, the company opened their first restaurant at 353 Main Street where it began as a lunch and ice cream counter. They originally made the ice cream for the restaurant customers only and then expanded distribution later. The Blake family ran the business up until 1998 when current owners Ann Mirages and Rick Wolsten-Croft took over.

Rick and Ann worked for Hood. Changes in the industry indicated there may be some possibilities on the horizon, so they decided to take a chance on Blake's when they saw it was for sale. Since they took over, they've probably seen an increase of about four to five times the amount of ice cream production than when they purchased the business. They offer over 80 flavors and distribute beyond New Hampshire into Maine, Vermont, and Massachusetts. All flavors are made on site except for the no sugar added flavors.

Ann knows that their ice cream has a "wow factor." They've been in the business a long time, and when she hears about customers' pleasant experiences, she knows that they're on the right track. Blake's participated in the Scooper Bowl – an event that takes place in Boston every year – which Ann saw as an opportunity to give back to the community and expand Blake's brand. In the three hours at the event, Blake's ice cream experienced a very positive reaction, which reassured Ann that they have a great product.

Blake's doesn't skimp on ingredients and, in the flavors that use them, add-ins. Ann talked about dropping in a pound of pistachios per batch. Dirty Water is Blake's first trademarked flavor and you'll understand the name if you're from the

Boston area. There is a basic coffee flavor, but as peoples' tastes have changed, they are looking for something stronger. Dirty Water offers that as a Colombian coffee base flavor which includes a chocolate cookie swirl and chocolate chips. Ann notes that "it's the consistency, it's the quality. Rick and I are very hands-on".

Graham Central Station has a plentiful and strong graham cracker flavor and Boston Blackout is a rich chocolate with a brownie fudge swirl and brownie dough pieces. It's quite possibly my favorite. Peanut Butter 180 is another personal touch – a reference to Rick's parents – and is unique due to the base flavor and all of the peanut butter add-ins. Some of the more unique flavors include Lemon Meringue Pie which is a lemon chiffon base with a graham cookie swirl. Cookie Jar is a vanilla ice cream with an Oreo and peanut butter cookie swirl. This is one of the best places to visit if you're looking for a huge number of flavors.

Red Raspberry Revolution is a red raspberry base flavor with a raspberry swirl and red raspberry filled cups. Graham Central Station is possibly the most popular flavor after Vanilla, as well as any of the chocolate flavors, Black Raspberry Chip Yogurt, and their Cookie Dough. Blake's creativity is a big part of the reason they are often approached by stands and restaurants who want to expand their offerings of flavors. They embrace the swirls (called variegates in the industry) in the ice cream world of today where variegates and add-ins are commonplace.

Ann's favorite thing about doing this job is the customers. "I love my customers and I love ice cream, the relationships you build and the connections [made]," she said. Her grandfather was an ice cream man, and while he was involved in ice cream long before Ann got involved with it, those experiences perhaps helped shaped her path into what it is now. Her love for ice cream has expanded what Blake's has to offer, and we've all come out winners.

Attractions in the area:

SEE Science Center, Manchester Historic Association Millyard Museum

Visit Blake's Restaurant & Ice Cream online at
www.blakesicecream.com
or they are located at
53 Hooksett Road
Manchester, NH 03104

Roselynn's Homemade Ice Cream

EPPING, NH

Roselynn's was opened up fourteen years ago by Joe Bodge, and is named after his children's middle names, Rose & Lynn. It started out as a glorified hobby while he was working as a mechanical contractor. He often made ice cream at his house for his friends. He had the building already at its current location, but it was being used for storage of antiques belonging to him and his father, and you'll see a few reminders of that around the eatery. They make their own base mix on site, which is fairly uncommon for a non-farm environment these days. Finding a pasteurized egg on a small scale for a small business wasn't the easiest thing for Joe either, but after the owner of a local company tried Joe's Black Raspberry ice cream, he changed his mind.

To complement the ice cream, Joe decided to open up a place with breakfast and lunch offerings. Joe's dad was a corporate manager for Friendly's ice cream and Joe himself worked for them at a young age before owning his restaurant. He loves creating and he has ninety-seven different flavors he can make, but generally rotates in about twenty or so including many vegan options, one of which is a vegan coconut chip with coconut milk and arrowroot. As Joe spoke about his Taylor 220 batch machine water cooling unit, he said: "It's a true old-fashioned ice cream. It has body to it; it has a lot of flavor. I know all the ingredients that are in everything." You'll notice right away what kind of flavor that type of commitment can produce.

Joe has lived in Epping for forty-two years, has served on the board for the town, and serves on the fire department. He brings in 150 pounds of King Arthur flour a week for his baking needs since they make a lot of baked goods on site. Mustard Vanilla, Cayenne Chocolate, and the Vegan Coconut Chocolate Chip are some of the more adventurous flavors they offer. Coffee normally wouldn't go under the spot where

I talk about unique flavors, but Joe says that his Coffee is unique. The reasoning is that it keeps you awake like regular coffee, as Roselynn's beats coffee crystals into the milk to start making the base. I love Coffee ice cream, but this one is different. You just don't normally taste this flavor as if it's an actual cup of coffee. I would suggest that some of you coffee lovers who don't normally like coffee ice cream go out on a limb and give this one a chance. Once a year in the springtime they do a single run of Strawberry Rhubarb Pie. They feed whole pies into their machine to make the base. A chocolate raspberry sorbet is sometimes available as well.

In a rare occurrence during my journey, Vanilla is not the most popular flavor. Here at Roselynn's, it's actually the Black Raspberry – and you know why when you taste it. Vanilla is down at number seven or eight on their list for flavor popularity. Toffee Butter Crunch is a butter base with heath bar toffee bits, and it was a very deep, rich buttery flavor. I also had a scoop of the Chocolate Mint which has this dense chocolate flavor. I'm already planning my next trip back so I can try the Chocolate Peanut Butter Swirl. They melt down chocolate into the milk and hand swirl in the peanut butter and it's a big hit. Mint Chocolate Chip is very popular at Roselynn's as well.

Joe's favorite thing about doing this job is socializing. He did well as a mechanic contractor, but was more interested in a social place that served food instead of a restaurant that was trying to churn out solid profits. You get the feeling that when you step through the door, you're walking into a home more than a restaurant. Joe doesn't distribute his ice cream as he can't control the quality and would never want to run the risk of someone being served frosted ice cream. They make their own cones, strawberry topping, pineapple topping, blueberry muffins for blueberry muffin sundaes, as well as breads and cookies. They are a year-round business and they do make ice cream the whole year as they have indoor seating. So, if you're tired of grocery store ice cream in the middle of winter, find time to make your way to Roselynn's, where you'll be treated like family too.

Attractions in the area:

New England Dragway, Star Speedway, O'Neil's movie theater. Hampton Beach is only twenty minutes away.

Visit Roselynn's Homemade Ice Cream at
153 Exeter Road
Epping, NH 03042

Smoke and Cream

SOMERSWORTH, NH

Anna had always wanted to be a chef since she was little and ended up going to culinary school. Originally, she wanted to specialize in pastries, but decided to take a more general food approach. Her first job was as a pastry chef at Corazon at Castle Hill in Austin, Texas when she was twenty. She ran the entire dessert section when her boss went to Brazil for the summer, so she had a lot of responsibility from an early age that would help forge her path to Smoke and Cream.

When she changed locations to Jonathan's in Ogunquit, Maine, they made their own ice cream and she took a real interest in that process. She learned a bit of creativity there and had the time to hone her craft in something she enjoyed and took a quick liking to. Anna Hafner loves French food and her partner, Tristan Maher, loves Asian-style food, but they felt that Somersworth wasn't a great spot for a French/Asian fusion style restaurant. A barbecue and homemade ice cream combo, however, did feel like it belonged in Somersworth, and so far, it seems to be working out.

Smoke and Cream uses limited natural ingredients and makes their ice cream in 8-10-quart batches. They don't add coloring to their ice cream, and Anna decided to work off of the desserts they serve. So, two of the flavors that were available when I visited were the Pecan Pie and the Banana Cream Pie ice creams, as those two desserts are served in their normal form at Smoke and Cream. Anna makes all of the ice cream from scratch, including their own cream base mix.

Smoke and Cream has a very limited ice cream menu. They only offer six flavors: Vanilla, Chocolate, Strawberry, the two previously mentioned, and the Blueberry White Chocolate Chip, which is the clear leading flavor at Smoke and Cream. They use local fruit from the area when it's in season to make their strawberry and blueberry ice creams. 45 Street Bakery across the street makes their pecan pies (and you should consider stopping in after your visit to Smoke and Cream as I've been there many times, highly recommended), while the banana cream pie is made on site. In the future, Anna would love to do a chocolate infused chili flavor and is interested in doing more risqué flavors. She also is thinking about doing a flavor suggestion box.

The other half of Smoke and Cream offers a pretty solid menu including pulled pork, pulled chicken, brisket, ribs and all of the typical barbecue fix-ins. I came here for lunch with my wife Tania and we're going back for the pulled pork and the absolutely amazing mac and cheese. They make their own barbecue sauces as well.

Anna loves the chemistry of ice cream. Starting with liquids and creating solids has a certain magical quality to it, and she recounted a culinary story of how crème anglaise and vanilla ice cream are pretty much the same things with the only real difference being the temperature it's served. Anna loves that she can take four ingredients and make something that everyone enjoys – "it's a wonderful thing."

The small batch process and in-house made quality is what will keep people coming back here. She even sources the eggs and milk locally. Smoke and Cream makes their own whipped cream, hot fudge, and caramel. Anna spoke of her children and how their greatest reward for having to deal with her running a restaurant is the tasty ice cream they get every day. When it's hot "there is something very special from spring to fall" that the "winter makes you appreciate the season more" and it may be a reason why we eat so much ice cream. She spoke about how no trip to the beach or the fair is complete without some ice cream, and your trip to Somersworth isn't complete without stopping at Smoke and Cream.

Attractions in the area:

Hilltop Fun Center, Bad Lab Beer Company

Visit Smoke and Cream online at
www.smokeandcreamnh.com
or they are located at
44 Market Street
Somersworth, NH 03878

The Common Man
SEVERAL LOCATIONS IN NH

Alex Ray started the first Common Man restaurant in Ashland back in 1971. Over the years, they've expanded to include over 15 locations and employ over 800 people. Prior to this summer, a single person made the ice cream for all of the Common Man locations, but now it's handled by a group of employees and after speaking with them, it was clear they all enjoy the work they do and the atmosphere they work in.

Alex is always down for trying new things, and Fabian Merrill who runs the commissary where the ice cream is created enjoys creating new flavors with the team of employees that surrounds him. They get their cream base mix from a local dairy. Alex takes a lot of pride in the ice cream they produce, and they bring in some of the best ingredients money can buy. Fabian says they're given the freedom to bring in the ingredients they need to make new things. One of those flavors is the Fluffernutter, a great unique flavor. If you love the classic peanut butter and marshmallow mix, this should be at the top of your list. Their Arnold Palmer sorbet is also something you won't see at many other places, if any. They brew their own tea for this unique creation.

The chocolate and coffee flavors sell the most after the Vanilla, which is the most popular flavor here. Moose Racks, Cookie Dough, and Caramel Sea Salt are all big sellers. Adam Sawyer told me they use salted pistachios in their Pistachio ice cream, and they feel it's one of the better flavors they have to offer. I couldn't disagree after trying it. During the fall months and holidays, they offer Cinnamon, Pumpkin, and Eggnog ice creams. They all enjoy their jobs in the commissary. They noted that they've heard stories from the Town Docks ice cream scoopers about the lines where people eagerly wait for their ice cream knowing how excellent it is. They make all their own yogurts and sorbets as well.

The Common Man is known for a few things, especially given their wide radius and number of locations. The Yankee Pot Roast is one of those things the restaurant is known for. For desserts, there is the chocolate brownie with caramel ice cream. Sometimes they have blueberry cobbler with their Aunt Ruth's Lemonade ice cream. Remember, there are quite a few restaurants and they are always changing the menus, so be on the lookout for new and exciting things.

The Common Man is well known for their support of community events and charities. They donate and work with the Make-A-Wish Foundation and they are involved with all the different communities where the restaurants are located. They also donate ice cream to CADY, a group connected to Plymouth High School which helps with alcohol and drug awareness.

Something unique to the Common Man is their team up with Plymouth State. Twice a year they do what's called Apprentice Ice Cream where the business professor assigns the students a theme for ice cream and creates teams to compete. The last few years the theme has been children's ice cream. The students come in and they create the flavors; they learn about the marketing and the costs. Every year the Common Man has an event called the Taste of the Common Man. During the event, each location offers a free taste of something that's on the menu. The teams from the Apprentice Ice Cream attend these events, and compete to see who has the best ice cream. The winner gets their flavor served at the Town Docks in Meredith. The last winner was the Lemon Raspberry – give it a try as soon as you can!

Common Man (and family) restaurants:

Comman Man Lincoln, Common Man Ashland, Common Man Concord, Common Man Merrimack, Common Man Windham, Common Man Claremont, Common Man Roadside in Hooksett, Common Man Inn & Spa in Plymouth (Foster's Boiler Room & Rise and Shine Cafe), Italian Farmhouse in Plymouth, Lago, Camp, Town Docks, and Lakehouse Grille all in Meredith, the 104 Diner in New Hampton, Tilt'n Diner in Tilton, and the Airport Diner in Manchester.

Squam Lakeside Ice Cream

HOLDERNESS, NH

If you have a day off and you're willing to take a nice drive, consider going on a trip to Holderness for one of the more beautiful views you're likely to find across the homemade ice cream map. David Moore bought the property and started the business in 1982. They were on the lake during the summertime and decided that it would be a great spot to sell ice cream. They bought some equipment, scoops, recipe books, put up a little building next to the road, and they were open for business.

"Homemade ice cream has a quality that can't be compared to store bought," said David. He knows even the average ice cream eater can tell the difference between the two, and that's why people make the trip out to Squam Lakeside. Summer is short, and people love to celebrate by going out for ice cream, and David believes this is part of the reason the state eats so much ice cream throughout the year. One thing is for sure, you're not going to walk away hungry from Squam Lakeside.

The bestselling flavors after Vanilla are the Chocolate and Black Raspberry. Cookie Dough and Oreo for the younger generations sell best and the Butter Pecan and Maple Walnut are big sellers for the older crowd. David tends to stick to the classics and simpler flavors. One of the more interesting flavors is the Swiss Chocolate which is a chocolate chip ice cream with malt. The malt isn't overpowering and gives it just the right amount of flavor balance. It's not quite like anything else I tried on my journey. If you can get your hands on the Black Cherry, it's superb and I recommend it. There are a lot of fruit flavors at Squam Lakeside, and Banana Cream is one of them. I finished my day with some Lemon Cream & Butter Pecan which was the right choice on a hot day.

Ice cream isn't the only thing that Squam Lakeside offers. They serve hot food as well. The typical Squam Lakeside outing for someone who doesn't plan on eating five to six different kinds of ice cream on their trip (like myself) would normally include the lobster rolls, handmade onion rings, and, of course, an ice cream.

David believes that while their location is unique, they try and impress upon their staff the idea that they are part of the experience. He asks them to put personality into their jobs, so when someone asks what their favorite flavor is, they should tell the customer what that flavor is as opposed to just saying every flavor is good. They employ local kids as well as foreign students who are in the area for school. David's favorite part of the job is the people. Getting to know who the people are, finding out how their day has been, and just interacting with the customers is a big part of the enjoyment he gets from running Squam Lakeside.

They have on occasions made special flavors for weddings or other events. Consider getting their ice cream for your next function. Squam is only open two and a half months, from Father's Day to Labor Day, so plan your trip accordingly, because it's worth the wait!

Attractions in the area:

Squam Lakes Natural Science Center, West Rattlesnake Mountain, Squam Lake

Visit Squam Lakeside Ice Cream online at
www.squamlakeside.com
or they are located at
1002 NH-25
Holderness, NH 03245

Squam Lakes Original Homemade Ice Cream

Featured in Yankee Magazine and voted Best in NH

Hard Ice Cream Cones or Dishes
Add jimmies or nuts for $.50

Kiddie Cone or Dish	$2.95
Small Cone or Dish	$3.95
Regular Cone or Dish	$4.95
Large Cone or Dish	$5.95
Colossal Cone	$6.95

Pints and Quarts
Hand packed "A pint to the pound the world around"

Pint	$5.95	Quart	$9.95

Soft Serve

Infant Twist	$1.95
Small Soft Serve	$2.95
Regular Soft Serve	$3.95

Sumptuous Sundaes
Hot fudge, chocolate, strawberry, ~~~ hot caramel, or peanut butter topped w/ whipped cream, jimmies or nuts and a cherry on top!

Kiddie Sundae	$3.95
Regular Sundae	$6.95
Brownie Sundae *Ghiradelli Double Fudge Brownie*	$7.95
Titanic Sundae	$8.95

3 scoops of ice cream each topped individually with topping, whip cream, jimmies or nuts and a cherry.

Frappes, Freezes and Floats
Have your dessert and drink it too!

Frappe a blend of ice cream, milk and syrup	$5.95
Freeze a blend of ice cream sherbet and soda	$5.95
Float a generous scoop of favorite flavor floating in the soda of your choice	$5.95

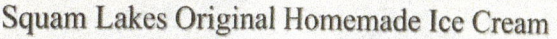

Vanilla	Chocolate Chip	Banana Cream
Chocolate	Pumpkin	Orange Pineapple
Strawberry	Black Cherry	Lemon Cream
Coffee	Coffee Espresso Bean	Butter Pecan
Chocolate Malt Chip	Peppermint Stick	Almond Joy
Rum Raisin	M&M	Black Raspberry
Peach	Swiss Milk Chocolate	Mint Chip
Oreo	Maple Walnut	Orange Sherbert
Coffee Heath Bar	Cookie Dough	Raspberry Sherbert
Reese's		Rocky Road

"You Deserve a Good Lickin"

Sawyer's Dairy Bar

GILFORD, NH

Sawyers has been operated from the same location for over seventy-five years. It was originally a dairy farm, and the Sawyer family eventually opened up a little shop that sold dairy products including ice cream. It was strictly a summer business, and it continues to be today. As they expanded over the years, Sawyers started selling hamburgers, hot dogs and eventually moved into seafood. Larry and Pati Litchfield purchased the business from the third generation of Sawyers, and it's worked out well.

The ice cream is made on site. Sawyer's operates at maximum capacity since they can only make the ice cream for three days a week due to their need for kitchen space to accommodate the massive amounts of people that show up during the weekend. It's a very busy location in a well-known tourist destination. It's due to this reason that they can't currently distribute, so if you're looking to check this one off your bucket list, you need to add Gilford to your map.

Sawyer's sells quality products, and they have a large batch freezer on site. Larry is a big believer in ice cream being properly batch frozen, and notes that massive ice cream operations have what's called a continuing flow operation, which can diminish the quality. "Temperature, fat content, humidity, and quality of the ingredients all factor into the taste of your ice cream," according to Larry. With the quality of ingredients being important, you should know that Sawyer's makes some of their own flavors here as well.

Two things bring people back to Sawyer's. First, they have four generations of customers due to their longevity in this one location; families and memories have been made here. Secondly, and much more obvious if you're visiting in the middle of July, it's a great location. Many people visit for some rest and relaxation in this part of the Lakes Region. Ideally, they are open for the season from Memorial Day to Labor Day, though they may open earlier and stay open longer depending on the weather and the amount of help they have to run the kitchen.

Larry believes their coffees and fruit flavors are outstanding. They do try to source some items locally such as fruits. They also make their own brownies for brownie sundaes. After Vanilla, some of the most popular flavors are the Black Raspberry, any of the coffee flavors, and the Sea Salt Caramel. I was a big fan of the Mint Oreo and the Strawberry Cheesecake. You should also consider the Red Raspberry Chip. One thing that sets Sawyer's apart from other parlors is their frappes. They sell thousands of frappes over the summer and they have a special frappe ice cream that makes their frappes creamier than your typical version. So, if you love a great frappe, you'll want to give these a try.

Larry's favorite part about the job is that it keeps him active and busy, and if you've ever been here on a Saturday, you'll know that he and everyone else working here have busy covered. Sawyer's is known for their seafood. It's all cold-water fish from the coldest parts of the world. They only purchase the best seafood. I had to go back later for some fried clams as I'd been craving them for the better part of a month and it was a bit of a wait, but be patient – it's worth it. They've introduced wraps and salads as well knowing the trend in healthier eating habits is in full swing, particularly with some of the younger generations. Regardless, you can come for the clams or the oysters, but you'll stay for the ice cream.

Attractions in the area:

Gunstock Mountain Resort (skiing, hiking, ziplines, and more), Bank of New Hampshire Pavilion (concert venue), Lake Winnipesaukee

Visit Sawyer's Dairy Bar online at
www.sawyersnh.com
or they are located at
1933 Lake Shore Road
Gilford, NH 03249

Arnie's Place
CONCORD, NH

If you're looking for a spot to have some pregame barbeque before your ice cream, check out Arnie's Place in Concord. I needed to eat lunch when I got here, and I went in not realizing it was a barbeque place – nothing like accidentally falling into a win. On the outside and inside, the restaurant has a fifties vibe. I assumed it was just a burgers and sandwiches type of joint, and it was, but I discovered it was more than that. The ribs here come right off the bone, and the pulled pork was very good as well. Tom's father originally managed a Friendly's and decided he could open his own place which was then passed on to Tom. Tom also has a love for the circus and that has its imprint all throughout the restaurant.

The Orange Pineapple and Indian Pudding (which consists of cornmeal, molasses, and ginger) ice creams are some of the more unique flavors you'll find at Arnie's. The Indian Pudding and the Pumpkin ice creams are seasonal and widely enjoyed. For me though, I came specifically for the Blueberry Pancake ice cream, and it was awesome. I have a tendency to seek out the more unique offerings beforehand and I wasn't disappointed with this flavor that I can't recall seeing at any other place I've visited. I decided to pair that with a Salted Caramel Chocolate Covered Pretzel ice cream. Why? Because that's what I wanted, that's why. One other flavor you may find of interest is the White Chocolate ice cream, which you could say is a signature flavor. I haven't seen that at many of my stops and there needs to be something to eat when all the real chocolate things have run out! Seriously though, it's worth a try. I enjoyed it since it was a bit more refreshing of a taste than I expected.

Vanilla unsurprisingly came in as the most popular flavor, but otherwise, the most popular flavors tend to be Coffee, Cookie Dough, Oreo and what seems to me to be the second most popular flavor in the state – Black Raspberry. I love this flavor so much. I remember trying this for the first time and can thank my dad for introducing me to it when I was quite young.

I asked McKenzie, an employee at Arnie's, what she loved about working at Arnie's. She went on to tell me, "It kind of feels like family cause we've all been working here a long time." Tom's favorite part of the job is the people he works with, which seemed to be a common answer among all of the employees I spoke to. You can tell it's one of those places where they all love coming into work. There is definitely a family atmosphere about Arnie's, and the customers must see that since business was nonstop the entire time I interviewed the staff. The customers seem to be a part of that family. It was obvious to me that many of the customers there during my visit were a loyal group of returning patrons and that isn't about to stop any time soon. According to Tom, the reason people come back is "the cleanliness, consistency" as well as the "great and friendly service." This is a model to follow for any successful business. I'd also add, however, that Tom is very hands-on and very involved in the daily business, and when people see an owner taking that much pride in their business, it's easy to support the establishment. They do wholesale to a few locations, but if you want Arnie's Place ice cream scooped for you, this is your only option, and a fine option it is!

ATTRACTIONS IN THE AREA:

McAuliffe-Shepard Discovery Center, Capitol Center for the Arts

Visit Arnie's Place online at
www.arniesplace.com
or they are located at
164 Loudon Road
Concord, NH 03301

The Puritan Backroom

MANCHESTER, NH

The Puritan Backroom opened in 1917 as a candy and ice cream shop. Arthur Pappas' grandfather started it. They originally opened on Hanover Street, and shortly after they opened a restaurant next to it in 1918. They had a full bakery as well until a fire in 1949. At one time there were seven locations, but the current property on Hooksett Road, which opened in 1938, now runs everything from this single spot including the restaurant and bar as well as the retail ice cream store. They even have a convention hall for party and event functions that seats over 200 people next door.

The restaurant is large, and you should come here hungry if you're planning on a night out. The food is amazing. I took my trip here during what I thought was a boring Thursday. It was raining out, and walking in, I thought my wife and I would be the only ones eating an 11 a.m. lunch. Fifteen minutes after sitting down, I looked up to see the place filling up, and by the time we were eating our meals, the restaurant was completely packed. The Puritan is known for their chicken tenders and mudslides. In fact, we were told that the Puritan is the number one user in the country of Bailey's Irish Cream for a single establishment.

At the Puritan, they make some of their bases including their espresso, chocolate, and strawberry. While that's great news, there was no way I was walking out of a place that serves Baklava ice cream without trying it, and it's an absolute must have. It's so flavorful with many different spices that are typically used in the making of baklava. It's not just spices though as it includes huge chunks of baklava in it. The Charlie Chocolate Factory is loaded with chocolate cookies, white chocolate chips, peanut butter cups, and brownie. While Arthur likes these flavors, he thinks that what really makes an ice cream place is the flavor of the mainstays such as vanilla and chocolate. According to Arthur, the most popular flavors behind the Vanilla and

Chocolate are "anything with Cookie Dough or Oreos in it."

People keep coming back to the Puritan because it's a well-known family restaurant and atmosphere. Arthur mentioned sixteenth birthdays, parties, anniversaries and other family events create memories, which bring people back later in life.

Arthur believes that "one of the reasons ice cream does so well in New Hampshire and New England is because we all have a sweet tooth." He did mention that parts of the country are too hot, and it melts too fast. He says some of their more troublesome days are when it's in the 90s. Ice cream sales directly correlate to temperature. This is true, as when its oppressively hot, many people don't go out for ice cream, perhaps subconsciously realizing it can affect their stomachs.

Puritan does sell half gallons of ice cream. Those sales also spike in the summertime, even when the windows were open; but, because they are open year-round, you can stop in and grab some in December. They make one batch at a time of ice cream in ten-gallon increments. Consistency and quality of the product help the Puritan stand out from other places – and the number of people there on my visit lends credence to that.

Arthur loves the work that keeps him busy here on a daily basis. It's something new every day, and he's very hands-on on the job. Since it's his family history, there is some self-applied pressure to continue the tradition and keep the place running smoothly. Opening a restaurant is not for the faint of heart, especially when you're making your own ice cream on top of it. The Puritan has over 200 employees between the Backroom, the takeout, the ice cream, and functions at the convention hall. It's labor intensive; but for him, it's entirely worth it.

Attractions in the area:

Palace Theater, the Mall of New Hampshire, SEE Science Center

Visit the Puritan Backroom online at
www.puritanbackroom.com
or they are located at
245 Hooksett Road
Manchester, NH 03104

Homemade Hard Ice Cream
made right here

Apple Crisp
Almond Joy
Black Raspberry
Black Raspberry Delight
Butter Crunch
Butterfinger

Carrot Cake
Cherry Vanilla
Chocolate Chip   *New* Chocolate Cookie
Chocolate
Chocolate Coconut
Coffee
Cow Tracks
Cookie Dough   *New* Ginger Ice Cream
Cookies & Cream
French Vanilla
Frozen Pudding
Fudge Swirl
Grapenut
Heath bar
Raspberry Sherbet

Kahlua
Lemon Sherbet
M&M
Maple Walnut
Mint Chocolate Chip
Mocha Brownie
Mocha Chip
Orange Pineapple
Orange Sherbet
Peanut Butter Cup
Peppermint Stick
Pumpkin
Pistachio
Red Raspberry Chip
Reese's Pieces
Salted Caramel
Strawberry
Tiramisu
Toasted Walnut Fudge
Vanilla
Soft Serve Chocolate
Soft Serve Vanilla
Twist

Waffle cones or cups $0.75 - $1.25 extra
Rainbow or Chocolate Jimmies $0.30 extra

No Sugar Added
Black Raspberry

Yogurt
Vanilla   Black Raspberry Chip   Chocolate Peanut Butter

Strafford Farms Restaurant
DOVER, NH

Strafford Farms is one of three family own restaurants at one location. They are open daily, and serve breakfast, lunch, and dinner. The Loft is upstairs and serves a great selection of beers and wines in a close-knit community pub-like setting. The Back 40 Grille and Ice Cream was my location of choice for this trip and I was surprised by what I found.

Strafford Farms opened in 1939 as a milk processing plant delivering milk around the region. The ice cream wasn't made during WWII for about two years, but otherwise, they've been churning it out for decades. In 1964, the milk processing machinery was sold to a Portsmouth company and the location transitioned into a full-time restaurant.

Strafford Farms was originally owned by the Rollins family, and then Peter Allen's grandfather bought it. Peter's father eventually took over, and then Peter continued the family tradition in 1993.

At first, the location served burgers and hot dogs. There was a seasonal window for ice cream but there was no inside seating. They eventually opened the restaurant downstairs, and it was renovated in 2004.

Peter makes the ice cream, though often times with the help of his brother and his son. Over the years, Peter noticed that the companies who sold ice cream flavors started increasing their use of ingredients such as corn syrup. So, Strafford Farms started making some of their own flavors such as their Butter Pecan (tasty), Apple Crisp (very tasty), and their Pumpkin – a seasonal flavor. One particularly unique flavor Strafford Farms makes is Carrot Cake. One evening at the restaurant, they were selling carrot cake as a dessert and Peter had some left over. He came up with the idea of freezing it, then taking it out, cutting it up, and mixing it in with his vanilla ice cream. It turned out to be quite a hit with the community and I only recall seeing this flavor at one other place in my journey, but not with chunks of cake in it the way Peter makes it.

Strafford Farms has a pint machine that was previously used for distribution, primarily for the creation of Hoodsie cups and pints for takeout. They now use it to do all their mixing for direct retail. Some of their more unique flavors include the Red Raspberry Chip and the Black Raspberry Delight. Of course, the Carrot Cake is the one that will likely have some driving across the state. The most popular flavor is once again Vanilla here, but Peter says "hot fudge should be eaten with coffee ice cream" – and I'd agree with that, but perhaps we're biased. I also sampled the orange sherbet, which is also made in-house and has a wonderful fresh taste. Lastly, I had a scoop of chocolate cookie on my way out the door. Strafford Farms hasn't distributed since the 1980s, so if you want their ice cream today, you'll have to come to the restaurant. If you plan on bringing a larger appetite, the restaurant is known in the area for their hand-carved whole bird turkey as well as their chicken tenders which they marinate, bread and hand-prepare themselves.

Peter likes operating the restaurant since there is something different to do every day, and he loves talking to the customers. Many of the customers are locals. Since it is an area favorite, Peter knows many of the visitors by name. Tradition brings people back to Strafford Farms, with its long history, and families wanting to share their experiences with their children and grandchildren. Things have changed so much over the years, but the one constant is the homemade ice cream and the family tradition.

Attractions in the area:

Willand Pond, Children's Museum of New Hampshire, Woodman Institute Museum

Visit Strafford Farm online at
www.straffordfarms.com
or they are located at
58 Rochester Road
Dover, NH 03801

GELATO
...and, well, that's different.

When I first started the idea of putting together a book on homemade ice cream, I hadn't considered gelato. I love gelato. Gelato is like the cousin of ice cream. There are only a handful of places that make their own gelato in the state, so I thought I'd add them into the book. I'll talk about the similarities and differences in a few of the following stories.

There were also a couple of places that didn't necessarily feel as though they fit into one of the other sections of this book – so I put them here. Jake's Old Fashioned Ice Cream isn't really a scoop shop, though you can go walk in and purchase a pint, and Chris' Wicked Ice Cream will scoop your ice cream, but it's the only place that has alcohol in every flavor you'll find on a menu.

VIBES GOURMET BURGERS

buza DAIRY BAR

GOURMET BURGERS — ICE CREAM · GELA

The Buza Dairy Bar

CONCORD, NH

Jeannette and Jim Zaza opened the Buza Dairy Bar in October of 2015. They started with the dairy bar, and then in November decided that a burger place would be the ideal addition alongside. While the Buza Dairy Bar does serve ice cream from Annabelle's, they specialize in making their own gelato. There is a perception that gelato is more fattening than ice cream. Gelato contains 70% less fat than ice cream because it's made with whole milk and a little bit of cream. It's also denser than ice cream because it has less air incorporated.

Jeannette has been an artist her entire life. She is a painter with a love of ice cream and gelato. Her respect and love for gelato meant so much that she studied gelato making in Bologna, Italy. The creativity of her art is worked into her gelato making and leads to the creation of unique flavors.

Jeannette believes that gelato is an offering not easily found in New Hampshire and that tends to draw people in. Some because they've had it in Europe, and others out of curiosity. She knows there are certain ingredients the locals prefer over others, but she does venture out on occasion to try new things. A well-liked unique addition, according to many of her customers, is the tiramisu gelato. This coffee-flavored treat which also hails from Italy finds itself as a perfect match with its cold treat cousin.

Jeannette grew up in California and they ate ice cream year round. Here in New Hampshire, many ice cream parlors close down for the winter. She's not quite sure what it is that makes people love the ice cream so much in the north where it's as cold outside as the ice cream we love eating. Jeannette noted that many "know that when March hits, even though if it's still cold out, people are getting ready to open their shops. It's something to look forward to after the cold winter." She does know that there are many homemade ice cream places in New Hampshire though, and it's likely a combination of nostalgia and love for things made from scratch that leads to so much consumption.

She loves having people try freshly made gelato and looks forward to the reaction of those who haven't had any before. The Buza Dairy Bar makes many of their own pastes (flavors already mixed) for the gelato as well, as they try to keep it as authentic as possible. It's not too tough to do since the ingredients are so simple. They do get a few specialty pastes from the company Fabbri out of Bologna, Italy, such as Amarena Chery. Some selections don't need a paste, like many fruit flavors. The fruit itself has a strong enough taste, which makes the paste unnecessary. Others she makes the paste for, such as chocolate, do have a bit of fat and sugar in them to help give the gelato some mass. The Buza Bar also makes their own waffle cones. Some are dipped in Godiva chocolate and sprinkles or nuts as well.

Jeannette gave me a quick lesson on making some Oreo gelato, and it's amazing how simple and quick it was to throw together. The machine made quick work of the product as well, taking only about two minutes to achieve a more solid form. She tells me that the Oreo is probably the most popular flavor at the dairy bar. Some of the best-tasting things in life are simplest in nature, and that holds true here. My wife, Tania, came along with me on this trip and Jeannette had a shamrock-style gelato ready for us and it was quite tasty. We held off on the gelato she had just made for us until after we grabbed our burgers.

Vibes Gourmet Burgers is the other half of their business. They have a nearby local bakery make their brioche burger buns daily, and the food is just as amazing as the gelato. These truly are the gourmet burgers you've been looking for and the flavors and combinations are quite unique to Concord, with one burger including New Hampshire maple syrup on it. One surprising find here is the poutine fries. In fact – one of their burgers includes the poutine fries on it! We finished with the Oreo gelato that was made for us earlier and the cold treat truly hit the spot. The taste is so cold and silky smooth it leaves you wanting more (which you can totally do and get away with considering the lower calories).

Attractions in the area:
New Hampshire State House, conservation lands, McAuliffe-Shepard Discovery Center, Capitol Center for the Arts, Red River Theater.

Visit the Buza Dairy Bar online at
www.vibesgourmetburgers.com
or they are located at
25 South Main Street
Concord, NH 03301

Bloomin' Cow

NEWMARKET, NH

Making ice cream has been something that Dawn Mirabella-Lewis has wanted to do since she was little. She grew up in the Bronx where there were many places that had a lunch counter and getting a small ice cream was part of the experience. She's always loved ice cream. A window of opportunity opened for her to open a shop, and she decided she wouldn't have the chance again. In 2011, she opened Bloomin' Cow Ice Cream and Gelato. She continued working her full-time job and made some time to attend the Penn State University ice cream short course. Dawn welcomed the challenge of producing ice cream as part of a business. She's now transitioned out of her old job and now works in ice cream and gelato full time.

Dawn believes that while gelato isn't well known in New England, people who have come to enjoy gelato are increasing in numbers. While I visited the parlor, I enjoyed the Ginger Beer gelato and a remarkable Cherry Vanilla Swirl gelato. This may be the only place in the state that makes their own ice cream as well as their own gelato.

One thing they do here that you may not find in other places is their big focus on non-dairy based (n)ice creams options, which are very popular with the vegan crowd. Bloomin' Cow also makes their own Sorbetto, waffle cones, and whipped cream. They even toast all their nuts for the ice cream and the toppings. Sometimes in the winter, they'll have a few hot meals such as mac n' cheese or chili. They also make brownies, cookies, and other baked goods, sometimes for use in their sundaes and ice creams.

I spoke with Eleanor Zwart who's been working at Bloomin' Cow for a few summers and she told me that the most popular flavor is the Coconut Stracciatella ice cream, which won an award for best ice cream of New Hampshire in 2017 from New Hampshire Magazine. The flavors are always changing out, sometimes due to ingredient availability, and they're constantly working with their sweeteners to provide the best taste experience for their customers. The peanut butter flavors tend to sell well in addition to the non-dairy based options.

When I visited the parlor, they had some very unique ice creams including Blue Sky (blue colored vanilla with lucky charms marshmallows), Peanut Butter and Jelly, and Blackberry Oreo all of which I enjoyed. Dawn told me about one she dubbed Triple A, which consists of Amaretto, Apricot, and Almonds.

"I think the important thing is to pay attention to your ingredients," Dawn said. "If you have high-quality ingredients from a good source, you're going to have an excellent product". Bloomin' Cow has spent a lot of time and money finding what they believe to be the best ingredients. Dawn is very proud of their coffee flavored ice creams as they've spent much time refining the product for the perfect taste.

Eleanor loves the cheery crowd that comes into the shop every day. Customer appreciation comes at the top of the list and Dawn would like to expand and create her own cream base mix eventually. As of the time of this writing, she is looking to open a second shop in the Ridge Marketplace in Rochester. I can only hope that the Dulce De Leche or the Amaretto Chocolate Cake flavors will be served there because that's on my "get again" list, and it should be something you look for as well when you visit Bloomin' Cow.

Attractions in the area:

Newmarket Mills, Schanda Conservation Park, Deciduous Brewing Company

Visit Bloomin' Cow online at
www.bloomincowicecream.com
or they are located at
55 Main Street, 1st floor
Newmarket, NH 03857

Sub Zero Ice Cream

NASHUA, NH

Growing up, my brother and I hung out with a fun friend named Bill Cassidy. Bill was a huge Ron Hextall fan, a former hockey goalie for the Philadelphia Flyers. On occasions, we'd play some street hockey and Bill was always the goalie. He had the equipment and everything. My brother and I were convinced he could be a professional goalie if he set his mind to it after displaying quick reflexes in a move that went down in history as the immaculate save. In his haste to get ice cream into his mouth, some of it fell. The piece of ice cream seemed destined for a filthy rug when all of a sudden Bill's lightning quick reaction managed to catch the piece of ice cream with his spoon. In few instances has a save been made in such a time of desperation. If you're looking for some of your own amazing ice cream reactions to talk about, you should consider Sub Zero Ice Cream your next stop.

Rita McCabe used to work for BA Systems in export compliance. Her husband, Mark, still works there as a quality engineer. They saw Sub Zero on a television rerun of Shark Tank, a show where people try to sell or get investments for their inventions. They thought it was awesome, but they couldn't find anyone near them doing it. Looking into it more, they found it was a franchise, and thought maybe they'd get involved in making ice cream the Sub Zero way. They flew out to Utah, ate at some of the shops, and while they were talking with the CEO, he got the call he'd been waiting on for six years – his process patent had been approved. Rita and Mark figured it was a sign and they opened their own shop in August of 2014 in Nashua, NH. As New England Area Developers, they are now looking for franchisees who would like to open their own Sub Zeros across the region.

Like many parlors, they purchase their ice cream mixes; however, unlike many of these parlors, they have options for those who are vegan or those who have allergies – an option not available at many parlors. In

Sub Zero, you pick from eight different base creams. They offer a premium 14% butterfat ice cream, a low-fat 5%, custard, yogurt, no sugar yogurt, lactose-free, soy or cashew milk. They also have an Italian ice base. For those with allergies, they'll actually pull the mix-ins out of the original boxes as opposed to using the mix-ins bar to avoid any cross-contamination. Rita says, "It's one of the first questions we ask – have you ever been here before and do you have any allergies?" Rita pointed me to allergyeats.com where they have a very favorable rating and reviews that you may be interested in reading through if you have allergies.

Since you pick your cream and then add your flavors – a selection of over fifty (most of which are not syrups but proprietary flavors, meaning many of the mixes have less sugar than other establishments) – you can create truly unique ice creams that you won't find at other places. The mixture is then individually flash frozen with -321 degrees Fahrenheit liquid nitrogen in a blast of chilled fog. This creates fresh, smooth, ultra-creamy ice cream. Rita recounted one younger customer who decided to go with a Bubblegum and Siracha mix. Good luck finding that opportunity elsewhere. Even though they encourage trying your own original creation, Vanilla still tends to be their most popular flavor.

Rita believes that tourism during summer months helps bump up the amount of ice cream that New Hampshire tends to eat. To keep business coming year-round, they have an indoor facility which also has a party room. In addition to this, Sub Zero is constantly outside of their shop for weddings, bar mitzvahs, corporate functions, school STEM enrichment programs and other events all over New England. They get a lot of enjoyment out of visiting schools and teaching science while following it up with a sweet treat for the children. They also do a lot of work with the VFW, Boy Scouts, and Girl Scouts.

My wife wanted to come with me for this trip because it's different – it's a show. She ended up going with the Bernoulli Brulee which is a Caramel, Vanilla, Cinnamon, Dulce de Leche mix with Twix and Heath. I myself decided to create my own Chocolate Cheesecake with Pecan mix. It's a fun process to watch the liquid nitrogen create your ice cream before your eyes. Rita loves that people come in with interest and curiosity and leave with smiles on their faces with an understanding of the science and process. "It's the only ice cream shop where you come in and there's no ice cream [pre]made. We create exactly what you want to order," Rita said.

Ice cream isn't the only thing that Sub Zero makes. They also make their own waffle cones, pies, cakes, and steamers (no not those steamers). These are basically cups of gourmet hot chocolate which is a nice complement to ice cream. Use science as an excuse to check out Sub Zero and eat some ice cream right away!

Attractions in the area:

Fun World, Launch Trampoline Park

Visit Sub Zero Ice Cream online at
www.subzeroicecream.com
or they are located at
495 Amherst Street
Nashua, NH 03063

Jake's Old Fashioned

NASHUA, NH

Roni Vetter runs Jake's Old Fashioned Ice Cream & Bakery, which is an ice cream distributor that makes super premium ice cream, sorbet, cakes, pies, and other baked goods. Jake's does have a retail portion that is small as they're a bit underground, which is actually a cool feel. At this location, they sell some of their ice cream in pints and take orders for custom ice cream pies and cakes. Jake's has been in Nashua at this location since 2013. The retail store opened in 2004, but they switched to a distribution model at the end of 2013 due to lack of space and wanting to sustain themselves as a full-time brand during the offseason. Jake's popularity was strong enough that Roni was able to turn that success into the distribution format she uses today. A former pastry chef with Ritz Carlton, Roni decided to branch out in a different direction and Jake's previous owners were looking to sell during this time. Roni said with Jake's "I could incorporate my pastry knowledge and dessert knowledge into my ice cream and branch off from ice cream and tie them together."

The majority of the ice cream used at Jake's is a sweet cream base. Roni tries not to dye any of her ice cream if she can help it and uses many natural ingredients instead. This can sometimes be a challenge, but she has a few tricks up her sleeves such as using natural fruit purees to change the color. Jake's direct distributes to most of their clients, which go as far north as Concord, as far west as Goffstown and Milford, east to Candia and south to Salem – about a 30-mile radius, on average. Their largest market tends to be with AG (Associated Grocer) markets, though they aren't in all AG locations.

Maple Walnut Bacon was presented to her by Kevin from KC Rib Shack in Manchester. He wanted an ice cream like that at his shop, but Roni wasn't sure how it would go over. They make some in pints for the store, and it's specially made for one of

Nashua, NH 603-594-2424
jakesoldfashionedicecream.com

their distribution points. The ice cream is now a hit, so give that a shot if you have the chance. While their Vanilla is popular it is outsold by both their Darkside and their Mint Madness. Darkside, a chocolate ice cream with dark chocolate chunks and fudge swirl, is amazing. I know because I took some home with me, and Mint Madness is mint chip and Oreo together, which is quite tasty. I can't recommend either of these flavors enough and they are well worth picking up if you're in the area or at one of the markets carrying Jake's products. I brought some home to have with family and friends and everyone loved it.

Roni believes there are a lot of excellent mom and pop run ice cream places in the state and when combined with the summertime and tourism seasons, sales of ice cream are prominent in New Hampshire. She also points out from her time working with the retail scoop shop that as the season starts ending, certain customers would come in less often, but when they came in, they'd start buying pints and quarts to take home. This is perhaps why I've found scoop shops that have switched to distribution or include distribution in addition to their scoop shops.

Don't forget that Jake's Old Fashioned Ice Cream & Bakery is also a bakery! The ice cream cakes and pies, while not unique by name, are unique in makeup. Roni creates made to order pies and cakes so it's truly unique based on what you as a customer want. Jake's has a guideline menu, but people are free to tailor make their orders.

Also, with Jake's ice cream cakes, they will make actual flour cake for part of the ice cream cake, which isn't exactly common these days as most people recognize ice cream cake as just ice cream with that layer of chocolate crunchies we all love, and some kind of icing. At some of the farm stands they'll have homemade ice cream cookie sandwiches, which are fresh baked cookies with their ice cream which the kids absolutely love.

Roni misses the social interaction of the retail scoop shop, but she thoroughly enjoys losing herself in the work of the job and dedicating herself to getting out a quality product to as many people as possible. It's a trade-off that's paying off for Jake's, so perhaps you'll see it in a store near you soon!

Attractions in the area:

Mine Falls Park, trail network, streams, nature preserve, soccer fields, a view of the old mill buildings, downtown Nashua.

Visit Jake's Old Fashioned Ice Cream online at
www.jakesoldfashionedicecream.com
or they are located at
57 Palm Street
Nashua, NH 03063

Morano Gelato

HANOVER, NH

As one of the few gelato places on my tour of New Hampshire, I was delighted to find my way to the college town dessert establishment of Morano Gelato after a long day of travel in which the temperature never dropped below 80. That made it much easier to look forward to a cold offering of some of the best gelato around.

Morgan Morano opened up in 2010 and started selling at the Hanover Farmer's Market. At the time, her gelato was made in a private school kitchen. She grew up in the restaurant industry and went to culinary school after college. She spent six years in Italy on and off, and she worked for a gelato chef for a few months. Morgan saw places that made Italian desserts, but didn't see too many people making gelato. A few years later she moved to a place on Main Street and shared her space with a cafe, but she was glad to have a place to make her gelato on site. "Hanover is an amazing town, and most businesses that open here thrive." That's mostly due to Dartmouth College, but the area tends to be a vacation destination as well.

Morano Gelato makes their gelato from scratch on site every day. While the labor costs are high to maintain this quality, they do everything they can to keep your prices low. What is really important though is that the gelato you get is made that day, every time. They use high-quality ingredients from Italy and Europe as well as some that are locally sourced. Morgan loves ice cream as well as gelato. She's pretty sure that if she wasn't running a gelato business, she'd be running a soft serve ice cream stand. She loves a creamy ice cream and noted that whether people realize it or not, when they eat ice cream, they're letting the ice cream melt a bit before actually tasting it. Whereas, the gelato you taste right away due to it being kept at a warmer temperature.

Morgan said looking back on it, that she had a bit of luck opening when she did. No one was really making gelato, and also during that time, cooking shows and chef programs were exploding in popularity. She believes having something different during that time period really helped boost her business. More than convincing customers to try the product, Morgan tells me the spoons, which are classic small spoons typically served with gelato, get a bit of push-back. Most people aren't used to getting spoons so small. The cup size and pricing can be looked a bit down on as well – though in my opinion the ice cream segment of eating out is only just now starting to catch up with the rest of the food industry when it comes to quality over quantity, and you won't be complaining about the quality at Morano.

The Orange gelato pairs well with the Dark or Milk Chocolate gelato, so that may be worth a combo option for the more adventurous. I ended up getting Cioccolato Fondente (a very dense and very dark chocolate) with Crema Fiorentina, which is a vanilla custard style with citrus – think creamsicle. Some of the more unique flavors they offer are the Verona (White Chocolate Strawberry) and the Cioccolato e Peperoncino (Chocolate & Red Pepper). The most popular flavor by far is the Cioccolate Fondente.

If you're new to gelato and only testing the waters, you won't find vanilla. What you're looking for is the Fior di Latte, which is a sweet milk, and about as close as you'll get to vanilla. Please note that because each flavor is made fresh every day, not every flavor will be available every day. Morano Gelato does offer an Affogato, which people really love. This is a coffee flavored dessert which usually involves a scoop of vanilla gelato with a shot of espresso on top.

Morgan loves seeing people enjoy the products she creates. She remembers eating out when she was younger and hearing people talk about how great food was at one place or another. Morgan dreamed about doing something like that when she had the opportunity. Morano Gelato does not distribute, but they do have a gelato cart which they take out to events in the area. "We are a company dedicated first and foremost to creating the best gelato we can produce."

Attractions in the area:

King Arthur Flour's Vermont Campus, Connecticut River, outdoor activities such as hiking and skiing, Lou's Restaurant & Bakery.

Visit Morano Gelato online at
www.moranogelato.com
or they are located at
57 South Main Street, Suite 101
Hanover, NH 03755

Frisky Cow Gelato

KEENE, NH

Linda Rubin has been addicted to gelato since she was twenty-three, and first tried it in Florence, Italy after waiting in line for an hour. Linda's association with Stonewall Farm in Keene is what really kicked off the idea of making gelato herself. She moved to the area twenty-five years ago, and her first job was at Stonewall Farm where she worked for nine years. She left for a few years, and when she came back, she joined the board of directors at the farm and led a campaign to start a creamery there. Now she makes her gelato in that creamery. Frisky Cow will forever be linked with Stonewall Farm. Linda believes it's important for people to have easy access to a working farm, and that's what the farm provides. In addition to being an educational center and a place to see farm animals, it also serves as a venue for events, where Linda's own son was married. Linda knew that when she started a business, she wanted it to be the type of business where some profits were giving back to Stonewall Farm.

She's always been a foodie. There is a lot of ice cream in New Hampshire which Linda fully admits she loves, but she was also looking for a healthier option. Most of the flavors she makes herself from scratch and she gets things locally as much as possible. She uses a blend of coffee called Coffee House Jive from Prime Roast located in downtown Keene for her gelato. Linda is clearly community driven, and Keene is benefiting from that.

Linda went to Carpigiani Gelato University in Anzola dell'Emilia, near Bologna, Italy where traditional gelato makers teach people how to create the much-loved cold treat. Linda knew quite a bit already through self-teaching, but the class helped her fill in the gaps or improve on things she was doing. Milk, sugar, and dried milk (solid/sugars/liquids) is the combination needed to make the base mix for gelato – and like ice cream, you need a proper mix to achieve the right texture. Linda is so detailed that she's changing her recipe based on the buttermilk from the cow's production because it changes throughout the months and as seasons change.

Frisky Cow was created only in March of 2018, but the initial feedback has been great. The most unique flavor Linda has created so far is the Blueberry Basil, another Italian inspiration. I told her that was a brave flavor to attempt and asked if the customers were just as brave; she said they were. Frisky Cow's more popular flavors tend to be Vanilla Stracciatella, Belgian Chocolate, Strawberry and Sweet Maple Cream – a perfectly balanced flavor. Linda gets the maple syrup from Ben's Sugar Shack in Temple. I had the Blackberry and Frisky Cow's signature flavor – the Stonewall Farm Heifer's Delight which is a cookies and cream that has a chocolate icing-like topping and sprinkles. I highly recommend a very strong flavored Salted Caramel as well. If you're dairy free, try the sorbetto. I had the Lime and it was amazing.

If you're curious why the tool for the gelato looks flatter than an ice cream scoop it's because the gelato is served at a warmer temperature. It's easier to scoop with a traditional Italian spade, and, in addition to this, they also serve your gelato with the traditional smaller spoon. Linda purchased

a display case specifically made for gelato for use at the farm and does cater for some of the farm's events. Linda also takes a gelato cart out to some community events.

Stonewall Farm is a non-profit education center. There are trails, and before I stopped here with my friend Darryl, we stopped over at the farm itself to see the cows and horses.

"Before I did this, I was the director of a healthy community initiative called Healthy Monadnock," said Linda, and one her focuses was "changing food environments to have more healthy options". So, she loves that she is creating a combination of her love for gelato making with her personal interests in local health and food systems. Frisky Cow is a benefit corporation which has a triple bottom line – she'd like to profit but also do good for society and the environment. Everything she has done before this has led to her doing this one thing that matches all of her values, and you're the one that gets to benefit!

DISTRIBUTION SIDEBAR: Luca's Mediterranean Cafe, Monadnock Food Co-op, CCDS Kitchen Market

Attractions in the area:

Cheshire Rail Trail, which runs from Walpole to the NH/MA border, numerous swimming holes included but not limited to Goose Pond, Wilson Pond, Otter Brook Lake, Surrey Mountain Lake, and Spofford Lake. Keene is a cryptocurrency friendly city.

Visit Frisky Cow Gelato online at
www.friskycowgelato.com
or they are located at
242 Chesterfield Road
Keene, NH 03431

Chris' Wicked Ice Cream

MILFORD, NH

Chris Perry was attending the New England Brewfest in 2014, and, while attending, he was invited to the Smuttynose 20th Anniversary Party. For the party, he decided to make some ice cream made with beer and the response was so overwhelming at the event that Chris realized he had discovered an untapped market. In 2015, he started perfecting his craft – going to festivals and selling the ice cream. Chris has been homebrewing since he was twenty-one, and has been creating ice cream for some time as well, so it was a natural fit.

The only scoop shop where Chris' Wicked Ice Cream is available is the Dessert Bar, which sits in the back of Barley & Hops in Milford. They work closely with Kelsen Brewing Company and change out flavors, rotating seasonally. They keep the flavor menu intentionally small due to the costs of the ingredients. This is definitely what I would call a refined product because the flavors are so unique; there is a big effort towards creating consistency.

In the fall, they'll have pumpkin flavors and sometimes they'll run flavors with specialty brews. They're always experimenting. Maple Bacon Bourbon is their newest creation, and it was worth the hour-plus trip alone. At times they have a Fully Loaded Margarita Sorbet. For their Pumpkin, they use a Shipyard Smashed Pumpkin with home baked cinnamon pie crust in it. They also made an eggnog this year which is a half eggnog, half sweet cream mix and then they add with rum added in and it's basically just like drinking eggnog...except you're eating it.

Vanilla Bourbon and Chocolate Bourbon are always on the menu as they tend to be the most popular with the repeat customers. They did have a Kelsen Stout flavor while I was on my visit, which has been uncommon of late. The Vanilla Bourbon is one people love to bring home and put on apple pie. They use Ghirardelli chocolate for the

Chocolate Bourbon. Some of the beers Chris was originally known for incorporating into his ice cream were the Draken Robust Porter, Paradigm Brown Ale (unavailable to acquire lately), and the Double IPA for his sorbet.

Chris's favorite part of the job is dreaming of flavors and then making them. They have no restriction on what they can make. At one point they tried a Pinot Noir flavor that some customers thoroughly enjoyed. On your way out of the store, you can pick from a selection of over 600 types of beers, over 450 singles as well as any homebrewing supplies. In case you're wondering, there is a provision in the food alcohol code for the state of New Hampshire for the use of alcohol in food, and if you're using between .05% and 6% alcohol in your food, there is no licensing required as long as the product being used was taxed, and those being served are twenty-one years and older.

Chris notes that you don't tend to taste the alcohol in quite a few flavors but more the malt; though they each still hold their own characteristics. The bourbon flavors and their Coffee Irish Cream come through with a much stronger alcohol flavor, and in the case of the Coffee Irish Cream, a strong aroma. If you're a lover of both ice cream and beers, this is quite possibly where you'll find heaven on earth. They take the time to do it right here, and you should take your time as well when you kick back with Chris' Wicked Ice Cream.

ATTRACTIONS IN THE AREA:

Bar One, Union Coffee House, Butternut Farm, Milford Drive-In Theater, Monson Center

Visit Chris' Wicked Ice Cream online at
www.chriswicked.com
or they are located at
614 Nashua Street
Milford, NH 03055

The Dessert Bar

Featuring  Chris' Wicked Ice Cream

also check out these...

I knew before starting this book I'd run into a few hiccups here and there. I knew it was possible and even likely I'd come across a few places where I couldn't connect with some of the owners for interviews – especially across a busy summer season where many owners are working and busy with their businesses. This doesn't mean I should exclude some great places I was able to visit, so here are a few condensed writings on places with amazing ice cream you should definitely check out.

The Ice Cream Machine

CHARLESTOWN, NH

Another great drive in the countryside may lead you to Charlestown, where I've tasted some of the best ice cream I've ever come across. All of the flavors here are top notch, and they have a nice selection of unique flavors as well. The Toasted Coconut is a homemade recipe that is unique to the Ice Cream Machine and it is well received.

I sampled my way through a few flavors here and the Creamsicle and Vanilla are excellent choices. I absolutely fell in love with the Bordeaux Cherry and I will be making the almost two-hour trip here again specifically for this flavor. The Molasses Gingersnap is amazing and tasted almost like the ice cream version of my own grandmother's molasses cookies – a must try, and a huge hit with the locals.

In addition to the excellent ice cream, the Ice Cream Machine makes their own sorbets. Brownies are made on site for the sundaes. They make their own waffle cones as well and have some of them dipped. I chose to go with Chocolate Brownie and Mud Pie on my cone and I recommend any flavor you want because you won't be disappointed with anything you get.

Attractions in the area:

Morningside Flight Park (hang gliding and paragliding), the Fort at No. 4

Visit the Ice Cream Machine at

213 Main Street

Charleston, NH 03603

Bubble Gum	Starry Night	Strawberry	M&M
Maple Walnut	Lemon	Cookies and Cream	Sugar on Snow
Butter Brickle	Chocolate Chip	Pumpkin Spice	Peppermint Stick
Mocha Chip	Cotton Candy	Mounds	Almond Joy
Chocolate	Coconut Raspberry Swirl	Grapenut	White Mtn. Raspberry
Mint Chip	Cherry Chocolate Chip	Toasted Coconut	Grandma's Apple Pie
Black Raspberry	Cake Batter	Orange Pineapple	Vanilla
Ginger	Rum Raisin	Cookie Dough	Chocolate Peanut Butter C

MINT   MAPLE   Open Daily 12-9

Ice Cold: C
Sprite, Su

Slick's

WOODSVILLE, NH

Slick's sits just on the border where New Hampshire meets Vermont. I spoke with my server Jenna Myers and she talked with me about some of the great flavors Slick's has to offer. Starry Night, which is a dark chocolate flavor with white chocolate chips, is a simple enough ice cream that still says, "This is something different." Bite This is a peanut butter-based ice cream with dark chocolate chunks and is one of the most popular flavors. Other popular flavors are the Mocha Chip and the Black Raspberry. If you're a fan of maple, give the Sugar on Snow a shot. It's a sweet maple ice cream with mini marshmallows.

Slick's give a great amount of product for the price here, which is a good thing, because you may want to go back for seconds. The Butter Brickle is interesting. It's a butterscotch ice cream with toffee pieces. Butterscotch isn't something you come across very often, so it was nice to see that. The Grandma's Apple Pie is a nice refreshing flavor as well. I got myself the Starry Night and the Black Raspberry. The chocolate ice cream in the Starry Night was just too dark for me to resist. It's likely you won't be able to resist coming back to Slick's. I certainly won't.

Attractions in the area:

Bath-Haverhill Covered Bridge, the Brick Store in Bath, swimming holes (The Big Eddy), Vermont – you can literally throw a rock from Slick's and hit Vermont.

Visit Slick's Ice Cream at

85 Central Street

Woodsville, NH 03785

Did I miss any homemade ice cream or gelato places?

I spent months researching ice cream parlors in New Hampshire before I hit the road, and even after all of that work, I'm certain I've missed a few homemade ice cream places. I did web searches, Facebook searches, and even went through the New Hampshire business registry to create my list. Many smaller town parlors that don't have a web presence might have been missed. Perhaps a place opened up after I did my research. There are three places I can think of off the top of my head that were told to me by friends or colleagues after I started writing. These things happen and if I missed something – it certainly wasn't intentional. If you know of a place or own a place that makes their own ice cream, please feel free to reach out to me at brian@brianeatsnh.com and I'll try and make an episode on my Youtube channel "Brian Eats New Hampshire" about your recommendation.

Stay up to date!

Watch my videos, read my blog, and follow my latest projects by visiting brianeatsnh.com. Brian Eats New Hampshire is part of Tasty Burger Productions LLC.

www.ingramcontent.com/pod-product-compliance
Lightning Source LLC
Chambersburg PA
CBHW081837170426
43199CB00017B/2754